Young People and Physical Activity

PROMOTING BETTER PRACTICE

Acknowledgements

The Health Education Authority commissioned a project team from the Department of Physical Education, Sports Science and Recreation Management to undertake a review of young people and physical activity.

The project was led by Len Almond and Sonia McGeorge with contributions from Carol Healey (HEA) and Bob Laventure (HEA).

The HEA wishes to acknowledge the advice and support provided by the members of the Young People and Physical Activity Advisory Group in support of the review process.

Elaine Burgess (Senior Development Officer, Sports Council)
Gordon Clay (HMI)
Ben Corr (Senior Leisure and Recreation Officer, Hull City Council)
Phyl Edwards (Sports Fair National Manager)
Peter Harrison (General Secretary, Physical Education Association U.K.)
Gillian Henderson (Sports Development Officer, Youth Clubs U.K)
Linda Lawton (Public Health Specialist, Health Promotion)
Mary Morris (Director, FitKid)

As a result of the review, two complementary documents were produced, *Young People and Physical Activity – A Literature Review* and *Young People* and *Physical Activity – Promoting Better Practice*.

The HEA is grateful to all those organisations and individuals who provided an insight into the needs and issues related to young people and physical activity as perceived by those working in the field.

In addition, the HEA wishes to thank all those who submitted examples of their work which are included in the case studies section of this document.

© Health Education Authority

1997

ISBN 0 7521 0702 X

Health Education Authority
Hamilton House
Mabledon Place
London WC1H 9TX

Typeset by Type Generation Ltd
Cover design by Tania Field
Printed in Great Britain

Contents

Appendices

Foreword

The health benefits of physical activity are now well documented. A wealth of research evidence now exists to support the promotion of physical activity, to improve public health. Consensus has been reached recently regarding the importance of encouraging adults to take part in physical activity, of a moderate intensity, on a regular basis. This has helped to give direction to the promotion of physical activity in England, and formed the basis of the HEA's *ACTIVE* for LIFE campaign.

Whilst such a consensus was reached with the adult population, the picture in relation to young people is more complex. In January 1995, the HEA commissioned a project team from Loughborough University to undertake a review of the research literature and current practice in the field of physical activity and young people.

This document has been produced as a means of disseminating the work of the project and provides guidelines to help a variety of agencies to take forward the promotion of physical activity for young people at local level.

This guidance document complements other work the HEA has carried out which supports the development of local interventions and projects designed to promote physical activity. It is intended primarily for health and local authorities and those involved in the promotion of physical activity for young people, but will also be of interest to those in teaching, the youth services and a range of agencies who work with young people.

Nick Cavill
Physical Activity Account Manager

Overview

This document has been produced to help professionals plan the development and implementation of a local physical activity initiative for young people by:

- identifying the important components in setting up such an initiative;
- providing examples from existing initiatives to illustrate how principles can be put into practice;
- encouraging collaboration between the relevant professionals, to provide a more comprehensive and coherent provision of physical activity opportunities for young people;
- providing key information on a range of case studies.

The case studies that follow provide a valuable starting point for those wishing to develop similar projects and interventions. They are based upon a variety of locally developed strategies to promote physical activity for young people. All the contacts listed have indicated a willingness to share their knowledge and experiences with other professionals, and are able to provide useful guidance on both the benefits and pitfalls of their unique and differing approaches.

The case studies are a detailed analysis of thirty local initiatives, preceded by a matrix providing at-a-glance information on each one.

WHO IS THIS DOCUMENT FOR?

This document is for all professionals involved in promoting physical activity to young people. It is particularly relevant for:

- physical education inspectors, advisers and advisory teachers;
- health promotion officers;
- leisure and recreation professionals;
- sports development officers;
- professionals in the youth service.

Although the specific priorities and agendas of these individuals may differ, they all have a common interest in promoting increased levels of physical activity among young people. It is hoped that this document will encourage the development of partnerships and joint initiatives between these professionals. The collective expertise, skills and resources resulting from such collaboration can help to develop more comprehensive initiatives which operate across a variety of settings and reach a wider target audience.

Physical education advisers and advisory teachers

There are statutory requirements for the provision of physical education within the National Curriculum; the non-statutory guidance highlights the importance of developing close links between schools and the local community that will help sustain life-long involvement in physical activity.

Health promotion professionals

The promotion of physical activity among young people is an important aspect of a healthy lifestyle and can have implications for both short- and long-term health.

Initiatives aimed at increasing levels of physical activity among young people are likely to make a valuable contribution to the achievement of some of the key Health of the Nation targets, in particular those within the areas of coronary heart disease and stroke, and mental illness.

Physical activity has a potential role to play in preventing obesity. This is particularly important as more progress needs to be made towards reaching the Health of the Nation targets in this area.

Leisure and recreation professionals and sports development officers

Such professionals have an interest in promoting participation in available physical activities, both on an individual basis or as part of formal clubs.

Initiatives aimed at young people are a valuable investment in the medium- and long-term as they are the customers of the future.

Youth service professionals

The inclusion of physical activity within youth work programmes can be very beneficial since such activity can positively influence young people's health; play a valuable role in raising young people's self-esteem and confidence; and provide opportunities for young people to learn about co-operation and leadership.

THE HEALTH BENEFITS OF PHYSICAL ACTIVITY FOR YOUNG PEOPLE

The health benefits of an active lifestyle for adults are well established. Research evidence increasingly indicates that young people who participate in physical activity will accrue both short- and long-term health benefits. There are clear indications of a need to promote physical activity to this age group.

Establishing an active lifestyle at a young age has been shown to be important in promoting a lifelong participation in physical activity, with early experiences influencing subsequent activity behaviour. It is clearly important for leisure, recreation and sporting organisations to attract young people in order to lay the foundations for a continued involvement in physical activity.

The promotion of physical activity to young people is an important priority for a wide range of organisations, and partnerships between such organisations can be beneficial in achieving the common aim whilst also helping individual organisations to address specific aims and priorities.

A summary of some of the main benefits of physical activity for young people is given below.

Short-term benefits of physical activity

Improved coronary heart disease risk profile

Physical activity has been found to improve blood lipid profiles in young people, and lower blood pressure in young people who are hypertensive. Lower levels of adiposity and improved glucose tolerance have also been recorded. Particular benefits have been found in young people who have high levels of these risk factors, but evidence supporting the short-term benefits of physical activity in this area are not yet conclusive.

Lower levels of obesity

Evidence suggests that together with a balanced diet and behaviour modification, physical activity (in particular lifestyle activities) can make an important contribution to reducing childhood obesity. It is, however, difficult to determine the precise effects of physical activity upon young people, since growth and maturation also influence body composition.

It is important to control obesity among young people as those who are obese are more likely to have cardiovascular risk factors, and may have a number of psychological problems.

Improved quality of life

Young people who are physically active have been found to have improved self-concept and self-esteem, and lower levels of anxiety and perceived stress. In addition, the improved fitness associated with high levels of physical activity enables young people to participate in a wide range of activities and to cope with everyday activities more easily.

Long-term benefits of physical activity

Reduced risk of cardiovascular disease in adulthood

An active lifestyle in childhood could play a valuable role in reducing the development of coronary heart disease risk factors. Research has indicated that cardiovascular disease may have its origins in childhood, and that those who develop elevated risk factors at a young age are likely to remain at an increased risk in adulthood.

Reduced risk of obesity in adulthood

Physical activity has an important role to play in the prevention of obesity and in the maintenance of weight loss. Young people who are obese are more likely to become obese adults and these have an increased risk of a number of long-term chronic health conditions.

Reduced risk of osteoporosis in adulthood

Evidence has indicated that physical activity during childhood and adolescence may have an important role to play in reducing the development of osteoporosis in adulthood.

Increased possibility of a lifelong participation in physical activity

Research indicates that those who are active in childhood and adolescence are more likely to become active adults. Since the health benefits of physical activity are well established for adults, it is important that active lifestyles are established early on and continued throughout life.

PHYSICAL ACTIVITY GUIDELINES FOR YOUNG PEOPLE

Although specific physical activity guidelines have been developed for adults it is more difficult to determine the ideal levels of physical activity for young people. Furthermore, imposing rigid guidelines may have a demotivating effect and make physical activity unattractive for young people. What is most important is to introduce them to a range of activities and provide them with enjoyable activity experiences which are likely to motivate them to continue an active lifestyle.

It is, however, acknowledged that individuals and organisations involved in promoting physical activity to young people need to have some indication as to how much activity they should be advocating. Two recent guidelines have been proposed which provide advice in this area. These are summarised on p. 5.

Children

The Children's Lifetime Physical Activity Model (see Corbin, Pangrazi and Welk (1994) in Appendix 4) focuses on total energy expenditure and the accumulation of physical activity. It suggests that children should:

As a minimum: participate three or more times a week in a volume of physical activity to expend at least 3kcal/kg/day, which is equal to the calories expended in 30 minutes or more of active play or moderate sustained activity, e.g. childhood games and activities; lifestyle activities such as walking to school.

As an optimum: participate three or more times a week in a volume of activity to expend at least 6–8kcal/kg/day, which is equal to the calories expended in 60 minutes or more of active play or moderate sustained activity, e.g. childhood games and activities; lifestyle activities such as walking to school.

Adolescents

Based on a series of comprehensive research reviews, Sallis and Patrick (1994) (see Appendix 4) have proposed that young people aged 11–21 years should:

- daily or nearly every day participate in a variety of activities which are enjoyable, involve a range of muscle groups and include some weight-bearing activity. The intensity and duration of this activity is not as important as the fact that energy is expended;

- three or more times a week participate in moderate to vigorous physical activity lasting 20 minutes or longer. Examples of possible activities include those using the large muscle groups as part of sports, recreation, transportation, work, school PE or planned exercise; e.g. brisk walking, jogging, stair climbing, basketball, racket sports, soccer, dance, swimming, strength (resistance) training, strenuous housework and cycling.

The above should be used as guidelines only.

PHYSICAL ACTIVITY LEVELS OF YOUNG PEOPLE IN THE UNITED KINGDOM

There is a need to determine whether young people are participating in sufficient levels of physical activity to enhance and maintain health and well-being. However this is very difficult to ascertain, as:

- the exact levels of physical activity required to promote the potential health benefits have not been clearly identified;

- there are a number of methodological problems associated with assessing physical activity levels among young people.

The limited evidence available indicates that many young people, particularly those of secondary school age, are not participating in the level of physical activity recommended in the most recent guidelines. Some studies have shown that children of primary school age are participating in the level of physical activity proposed in the Children's Lifetime Physical Activity Model, but these levels appear to be reached by accumulating many short bouts of activity, and the benefits of such short bouts of activity for children have yet to be substantiated.

Important messages highlighted by existing research include:

- young people are fit but not active;
- girls tend to be less active than boys;
- activity levels tend to decline with age.

Although more research is needed to accurately determine the extent of problem, indications are that there is a need to encourage more young people to be more active.

SETTING THE SCENE

Acknowledging the potential health benefits of an active lifestyle has raised the profile of physical activity and resulted in a number of important national developments. The most relevant of these are summarised below.

Physical Education in the National Curriculum

The introduction of the Physical Education National Curriculum in 1992 highlighted the importance attributed to promoting physical activity among young people. The Physical Education National Curriculum means that:

- physical education has become an entitlement for all children aged 5–16 years;
- teachers are required to provide all pupils with a designated range of activity-area experiences. Specific activity areas for each key stage have been defined together with statutory General Requirements;
- health-related activities are included as a statutory requirement at each key stage. Students are required to acquire the knowledge, understanding and skills needed to pursue an active life through practical experiences of appropriate activities.

The National Curriculum does not stipulate the amount of time to be allocated to physical education, and as many schools have only a relatively small amount of curriculum time for this subject, only a limited range of activity experiences can be offered.

The Health of the Nation

The Health of the Nation sets out a strategy for promoting health in England, with an emphasis on disease prevention and health promotion.

It also sets national targets in five key areas: coronary heart disease and stroke; cancers; mental health; HIV/AIDS; and accidents.

Physical activity can make an important contribution to the achievement of the Health of the Nation targets, although no specific targets are set for physical activity. For example:

- physical activity can act to reduce directly the risk of coronary heart disease and stroke;

- physical activity can play an important role in the prevention of obesity. This is particularly important as obesity can negatively affect coronary heart disease risk factors, has been identified as a risk factor for selected cancers and Type II diabetes and is associated with osteoarthritis and gallstones;

- physical activity may have a positive influence on targets for the mental illness key area. Promoting the psychological health and well-being of children and adolescents is highlighted as an important area within the Health of the Nation. Studies on adolescents have found that physical activity can have a significant beneficial effect on psychological variables such as depression, self-esteem/self-concept and stress/anxiety. There is increasing evidence that early effective intervention in childhood and adolescence can be important in preventing adult mental ill health.

It is acknowledged that establishing healthy lifestyles at a young age will be crucial to the long-term success of the Health of the Nation strategy, and the promotion of physical activity among young people was highlighted as one important aspect of young people's health at a Health of the Young Nation conference held in July 1995.

The Physical Activity Task Force

The Physical Activity Task Force was established in July 1993. The role of the group was to develop a comprehensive physical activity strategy for England, focusing on encouraging participation in physical activity among the adult population.

The Physical Activity Task Force have produced a consultation document, *More people more active more often*, which sets out proposals for this strategy. The document identified children as one special group whose particular needs need to be addressed at both a national and local level. Following extensive consultation, a physical activity strategy statement was launched by the Department of Health in March 1996. This also identified children and young people as a priority population group.

Sport – Raising The Game

In July 1995 the Department of National Heritage published *Sport – Raising the Game* which outlines proposals to encourage and promote sport, in particular through improved provision in schools and sports clubs. If adopted, the proposals contained within this document could provide more opportunities for participating in sport and regular physical activity.

Summary

All of the above developments have raised awareness of the importance of physical activity, and the promotion of physical activity is now placed firmly on the agenda as a priority for young people. The Health Education Authority National Campaign to Promote Physical Activity, *ACTIVE* for LIFE, aims to motivate more adults to adopt an active lifestyle and will give physical activity a very high profile. Although this campaign is initially aimed at the adult population, the widespread interest stimulated is likely to have a positive influence on young people.

A framework for planning

WORKING WITH YOUNG PEOPLE

There are a number of fundamental principles which should form an integral part of any strategy aimed at promoting physical activity to young people. These principles should permeate all physical activity initiatives targeted at young people, and should help structure the way in which opportunities are presented to ensure equity, fairness, respect for young people and consideration of others. These principles are essential to ensure that purposeful and enjoyable physical activity is made accessible to all young people and that participation levels are consequently increased.

Access

All children should have access to a range of physical activity opportunities which are appropriate and accessible in terms of location and cost.

Equity

All students, including those with special needs, must be provided with equal opportunities to participate in different physical activities and experience a sense of achievement in so doing.

Integration

Young people should have the opportunity to participate in physical activity with peers of varying levels of ability and aptitude. In this way they can learn to appreciate and value the abilities, the different types of achievements, the individual contributions and personal experiences of life that young people can bring to the physical activity arena.

Integrity

It is not enough to simply engage young people in physical activity; they should also be involved in acquiring a practical knowledge base. This will help enable them to participate independently in physical activity.

Breadth

Provision within a locality should cover a broad range of physical activities for young people to experience, so that they can gain an appreciation of what each has to offer. Each young person will have different needs, interests and abilities, and these will influence their choice of physical activities. If a broad range of opportunities is available, all young people should have the chance to find the type of physical activity that suits them best.

Balance

Physical activity provision for young people in any one locality should be balanced, with different types of activity each given sufficient attention. This will help enable all pupils to experience the benefits of diverse activities.

Coherence

There should be coherence both within a particular physical activity initiative and also within the provision of the locality. A strategy should be planned to embrace a rich variety of different experiences in a range of settings. It is particularly important to ensure coherence between physical activity in school and provision within the local community. Specific links and liaison between schools and relevant organisations in the local community are essential.

Relevance

Physical activity promotions aimed at young people should be relevant to the particular needs and interests of young people in the local area. It is important to take account of factors such as young people's previous experiences, their readiness for particular experiences, their interests, aptitudes and achievements.

Differentiation

It is important to acknowledge the need to offer differentiated tasks in order to cater for a wide range of abilities, needs and interests. This is important if all young people are to be catered for, and will require a variety of teaching and learning approaches and organisational management.

Summary

The above principles should underpin all physical activity provision for young people. Essentially, there are two central issues:

- every young person can be 'good' at physical activity;
- every young person has the right to positive physical activity experiences.

Principles into practice

If these two issues are to be addressed, those organising young people's physical activity experiences need to:

- involve young people in the planning and provision of activities and value their contributions;

- address the specific needs of young people;

- respect young people as individuals with differing experiences, capabilities and preferences;

- provide opportunities which are fun, enjoyable and challenging; this may involve providing differentiated options to enable all young people to participate at their own level;

- encourage individual responsibility by providing young people with the confidence, capability and skill to move from dependence towards independence, and so enable them to maintain an active lifestyle;

- respect young people who have specific cultural and religious conventions;

- praise, encourage and motivate young people, and recognise any improvements they make;

- focus on personal improvement;

- reward effort and ensure that success is possible for all young people;

- take account of the impact of gender and maturational differences;

- provide positive and corrective feedback, in private if appropriate;

- consider groupings of young people carefully;

- ensure that young people involved in contact-sports and competitive activities are matched appropriately.

YOUNG PEOPLE AND PHYSICAL ACTIVITY – A STRATEGIC APPROACH

Figure 1 shows the key components of a strategic approach to promote increased participation in physical activity by young people at a local level. This is followed by brief practical examples illustrating how particular steps have been addressed by existing initiatives. Further key information on the examples mentioned is provided in the case studies section in the second half of this document.

All of the contacts featured in the case studies are willing to share their knowledge with colleagues, and their practical experience can help to provide a good foundation for those intending to develop similar initiatives. Although all initiatives will need to be adapted to take account of a particular locality's resources and needs, it is often possible to replicate the basic framework adopted by others, utilising ideas from a range of other initiatives.

The promotion of physical activity for young people has relevance for many organisations at a local level and it is recommended that these organisations work together to produce a comprehensive and coherent local physical activity strategy for young people.

Figure 1: A framework for planning a physical activity initiative

Modified from *Promoting physical activity–Guidance for commissioners, purchasers and providers.* Health Education Authority 1995.

STEP 1. CONDUCTING A NEEDS ANALYSIS

Conducting a needs analysis can seem time consuming and expensive. However, the information gained will be very valuable in helping to justify the commitment of funding to initiatives; and will help to ensure that initiatives effectively address the specific needs in the locality.

Any proposed interventions at a local level should address an identified need within the locality and be structured to match the specific needs, preferences and priorities of the target group. In order to ensure that this is the case, it is important to carry out a needs analysis, using both national research data and information on local trends, focusing on:

- establishing whether or not there is a need to increase the participation levels of young people in the locality;
- identifying the specific physical activity needs of young people in the locality.

Is there a need to increase levels of physical activity?

National information

The first stage of a needs analysis should consider the national information that is available, in particular relevant research reports from universities and the OPCS and Sports Council. National research evidence:

- suggests that young people are not currently participating in sufficient physical activity to acquire the potential short- and long-term health benefits;
- has identified a particular need to increase activity levels among young people who have a disability, or are female, or are from a black or minority ethnic group.

Local information

Information on local physical activity patterns and levels is essential to establish whether general participation trends are reflected in a particular locality; and to determine whether any specific groups of young people in the locality appear to be particularly inactive.

In some cases, local data may already be available from existing surveys. If this is not the case an appropriate survey should be conducted to gather this information.

What are the specific physical activity needs of local young people?

Initiatives will only be effective if they address the particular needs of this age group. It is also important to recognise that this is not a homogenous group and that needs may vary between different sub-groups, with factors such as age, gender, ethnicity and social class likely to have an influence.

National information

An analysis of the research studies available will provide useful indicators for those involved in planning a local initiative. For example research has indicated that:

- young people like to have the freedom to choose from a wide range of physical activities;
- young people tend to prefer activities which are fun and enjoyable and do not require a high level of exertion;
- factors such as accessibility, cost and the existence of appropriate support structures contribute greatly to young people becoming more active.

Local information

The physical activity needs, preferences and priorities of young people are influenced by numerous factors and each locality will have its own unique set of circumstances affecting these factors. A local survey:

- will provide an insight into the specific physical activity needs of young people in a particular area;
- is valuable in determining priority areas;
- will help to highlight the type of interventions likely to be most effective.

Practical methods of obtaining useful information in a relatively short period of time need to be identified. Ideally surveys should collect data on both current physical activity levels and needs. It can be helpful to adopt surveys used by colleagues in other regions. Local focus groups which involve young people can help to provide further information. There follows three examples of how information was gathered and how it led to local initiatives.

> ### Case study 1 – Survey and Audit Projects – East Berkshire
> The Community Leisure Services Unit in the Royal Borough of Windsor and Maidenhead in conjunction with the East Berkshire Community NHS Trust, undertook an audit of provision and providers of sport for young people. In addition the two organisations collaborated on an 11-school survey of the factors affecting participation in physical activity and the perceptions and attitudes of young people. *See* p. 48.
>
> ### Case study 2 – Fitness Survey by Waveney District Council
> In association with the Health Education Authority and Lowestoft College, Waveney District Council carried out surveys in schools to obtain local data on young people's fitness levels and information on their lifestyle. The survey was preceded by a consultation and planning period, and a pilot survey was carried out. Data was collected from young people aged 8–14 years using fitness assessments, a questionnaire and a food diary. *See* p. 50.
>
> ### Case study 4 – Health and exercise clubs for young people, Mendip District
> Prior to introducing a mobile Health and Exercise Club for young people aged 14–18 years, Mendip District Council carried out a consultation on the current exercise habits, fitness levels and perceived needs of this age group within the district. A brief questionnaire was administered and discussion groups were used with young people in a local school. It was hoped that this consultation would help to ensure that the clubs specifically addressed the needs of the local young people, were perceived as fashionable and were sensitive to the young people's physical limitations. *See* p. 53.

STEP 2. CONDUCTING AN AUDIT

The information obtained from an audit can complement the data from a needs analysis, helping to inform strategy and identify priorities. An audit should answer the following questions:

- What is the current provision of physical activity opportunities for young people in the area?

- Who are the current providers of such activities?

- What evidence is available to support the need to promote physical activity?

- Is there any relevant previous learning?

Audit of current provision of physical activity

Such an audit will provide an indication as to how well the needs of the young people in the locality are being met. Total provision within a range of settings should be considered, together with the type of provision and the accessibility of available opportunities.

Audit of active providers of physical activity

Potentially, there is a wide range of individuals and organisations who provide physical activity opportunities for young people across a variety of settings. Providers can include: schools; youth clubs; sports clubs; community organisations; leisure and recreation centres; commercial fitness centres.

An audit of providers should also consider their experience and expertise in promoting physical activity to young people.

Knowledge of physical activity providers within a locality can help to:

- identify the support structure available to help implement any initiatives;
- identify areas in which there is a training need (in some cases appropriate training may need to be carried out before initiatives are implemented).

The audit tool on p. 17 can be used to assess the provision in the locality.

Table 1: Audit of local provision of services and facilities

Group/facility:	How many?	Where?	How accessible to group?
Swimming pools			
Sports facilities			
Health and fitness suites			
School facilities			
Community facilities, e.g. halls, crèches			
Mobile facilities			
Conducive environments			
Cycle routes/tracks			
Designated walks			
Parks/playing fields			
Other open spaces			
Active local groups			
Sports clubs			
Sports promotion and development units/ sports outreach			
Private clubs			
Primary care			
Health promotion			
Local resources, e.g. LAY tutors, community sports leaders, crèche workers, exercise class teachers			
Promotion and publicity services			

The following examples illustrate how the information from a needs analysis and audit can be combined to help improve provision for young people.

Case study 5 – The Suffolk Sports Link Scheme

The aim of the Suffolk Sports Link is to develop sporting and recreational opportunities for students at upper/high schools and to increase participation in community-based activities. Year 10 students completed questionnaires, which revealed that many young people were interested in participating in sport but lacked information on clubs and facilities in the locality. As a consequence, an audit was carried out to determine current provision in the local area, and the findings of this audit were compiled in a directory, providing young people with ready access to information on available opportunities, and raising interest in activities. The information has also helped to identify appropriate providers to include in the Sports Link Scheme. *See* p. 54.

Case study 6 – Holiday activities organised by Arun District Council and West Sussex Youth Services

A questionnaire was given to young people aged 11–16 to identify the types of activity they would like to participate in during their school holidays. An audit of local provision was then carried out to identify existing opportunities which matched their needs and to identify gaps in provision. New activities were introduced to fill these gaps and a final programme of activities was published in a glossy, attractive brochure which includes comprehensive details about each activity, general details about the scheme, information on other local facilities and events, and free sports vouchers. *See* p. 55.

Audit of evidence

An audit of evidence is intended to provide a body of data illustrating the need for a physical activity strategy and is an important part of the process of gaining support. This audit should consider both the data available nationally and locally and could include evidence from: research reports; research articles in journals; reports from relevant national and regional agencies; survey reports.

Case study 7 – Making sense of health-related exercise: a guide for teachers, Swindon Health Promotion Unit

Swindon Health Promotion Unit have carried out a comprehensive audit of the literature pertaining to health-related exercise. This information has been used to compile of a pack for teachers on the 'what, why and how' of health-related exercise. Accompanying resources and relevant training will also be made available for teachers. *See* p. 56.

Audit of previous learning

Such an audit can help to save time; and provides a valuable insight into the strengths and weaknesses of different strategies and approaches.

It is particularly important to contact colleagues who have already had experience in implementing appropriate physical activity strategies to young people. The case studies outlined in this document provide a useful starting point.

Case study 8 – Sustrans Safe Routes to Schools Project

In Autumn 1995, Sustrans initiated a project to improve levels of health and fitness in selected pilot schools by improving safety for young pedestrians and cyclists and encouraging young people to walk and cycle to school. Prior to developing this Safe Routes to Schools Project, Sustrans conducted an audit of all similar projects. As the information available on similar projects in this country was limited, Sustrans extended the audit to include projects conducted abroad. Research covered projects in Denmark, Holland, Germany and America. Based on this audit a report was produced, outlining details of practice recommended for incorporation into any comprehensive United Kingdom project. *See* p. 58.

STEP 3. CREATING A FORUM AND STRATEGY TEAM

The formation of a relevant forum or strategy team early on is important to ensure that all those with an interest in the promotion of physical activity to young people are involved in discussions about a potential strategy from the planning stage. Forums provide the opportunity to consider ideas from a wide range of perspectives; and provide a good starting point for the initiation of relevant partnerships and networks. The involvement of young people themselves in such a group can be beneficial.

Not every member of this initial forum need necessarily become involved in the direct management and co-ordination of the subsequent strategy, although it is advisable that a core group continues to be involved at least in an advisory capacity.

Case study 9 – The Active Partners Project and Hampshire Physical Education and Sport Partnership

A recognition of the need to improve the quality of physical education in Hampshire Schools and to promote and develop pathways for students to increase their participation outside of school led to a conference being organised to discuss these issues. Individuals from relevant organisations were invited, with all levels of staffing included. The forum established a rationale, principles and ways of working which formed the foundation from which the subsequent Active Partners Project was developed. A relevant steering group has remained an important aspect of the Hampshire Physical Education and Sport Partnership which evolved from the Active Partners Project. *See* p. 59.

Case study 10 – Pro-Sport

Pro-Sport is a regional disability project aiming to provide the mechanisms through which people with disabilities can participate in sport. The project provides a consultation and co-ordinating service acting as a single point of contact, to which sports agencies can turn for advice on developing equal opportunities in their provision of sport. Central features of this project are a Sports Forum of Disabled People, which includes administrators, coaches, sports providers and sports people who have a disability, and a Young Disabled People in Sport Advisory Group. *See* p. 61.

STEP 4. DEVELOPING A STRATEGY

Underpinning any physical activity initiative for young people should be an appropriate strategy to ensure that needs are most effectively met. A local physical activity strategy should:

- consider overall provision in the locality;
- consider the priorities and preferences of young people in the locality;
- be developed with involvement from a range of relevant partners;
- be based on the findings of the local needs analysis and audit.

Physical activity promotion can form one part of more extensive strategies focusing on, for example, the achievement of local Health of the Nation targets or the reduction of coronary heart disease. A specific physical activity strategy helps to:

- ensure a coherent provision of physical activity across a range of settings;
- co-ordinate existing and new initiatives;
- encourage involvement and commitment from a variety of partners.

Following is a summary of the points to take into account when establishing a physical activity strategy.

A statement of the rationale: Including both the general rationale for promoting physical activity to young people and specific reasons for promoting physical activity to young people in the locality.

A summary of the relevance to partners: Including an outline of the importance and relevance of promoting physical activity to young people for each of the partners involved.

A summary of national guidelines: Including information on any relevant national guidelines. For example, the Physical Education National Curriculum provides clear guidelines for work in schools and the Sports Council has produced a document on young people and sport which provides advice on promoting sport in a range of settings.

Establish principles and values: The fundamental principles and values underpinning the strategy need to be agreed upon and stated. A consideration of the principles outlined on pp. 13–14 will help provide a basis for this.

State aims and objectives: These should be specific and measurable and should include an indication of the timescale involved for their achievement.

List partner contacts: This should include details of the most appropriate contact person within each organisation.

Case study 11 – Take Part in Herts
The strategy document for Take Part in Herts was compiled by the Physical Activity Advisory Group for Hertfordshire, a multi-agency group. The rationale for the strategy was based on national and local research indicating the prevalence of inactivity, scientific evidence linking inactivity with increased ill-health and relevant national and international health policy. The aim is 'To get more people more active more of the time', and a range of objectives have been set to help achieve this goal. A number of general principles have been established, including the promotion of physical activity as enjoyable and accessible for all, the elimination of discrimination, and the establishment of training to ensure consistent and informed messages in the field of physical activity. The role of schools, nurseries and playgroups in promoting physical activity to young people is recognised. *See* p. 63.

See also St Edmundsbury Bodycare Roadshow, pp. 15 and 51.

STEP 5. IMPLEMENTATION PLAN

An implementation plan should include consideration of the following points:

- key partnerships;
- priorities;
- settings;
- target groups;
- appropriate interventions;
- costs;
- training needs;
- identifying responsibilities and co-ordination of the initiative(s);
- identifying the most effective method of publicity to promote an initiative;
- identifying performance indicators.

Key partnerships

Partnerships involving partners from a range of key organisations are likely to:

- have more credibility and impact when implementing an initiative;
- be more effective due to the collective time, effort and enthusiasm available;
- have access to a broad range of expertise, skills and resources, more funding opportunities, a wider range of facilities and settings, more networks, and a more extensive support structure;
- help to prevent duplication of services and effort;
- help to improve continuity and co-ordination of provision.

Possible partners for initiatives include:
- local education authorities;
- health authorities;
- local authorities;
- youth services;
- voluntary organisations;
- Sports Council Regional Offices;
- institutes of higher education/universities;
- regional governing bodies of sport.

For further details of these organisations refer to the appendices to this book.

Partnerships which facilitate links between schools and outside agencies are particularly important to enable young people to participate in physical activity independently.

The relevance and importance of promoting physical activity for each of the partners should previously have been established in developing a strategy. There is a need to identify a shared focus which enables each partner to represent the specific needs and interests of their respective organisation. Aims, practices and procedures also need to be agreed upon.

Case study 12 – Ready, Teddy, Go – Manchester

Ready, Teddy, Go brings together a variety of key partners with the common aims of increasing the awareness among teachers, parents and children of the need for a more active and healthy lifestyle, and helping them to take appropriate action. The result of this partnership is an initiative that includes the provision of activity sessions for children and adults in the school setting by relevant local coaches and leaders (outside of school hours), the establishment of exercise sessions at the local park and the setting up of a healthy eating tuck shop. *See* p. 65.

Priorities

It is important to identify priorities in order that resources can be used most effectively. The information from the needs analysis and audits will provide indications as to the most important issues that need to be addressed. Factors likely to influence this procedure include:

- the resources available (finance, time, skills etc);
- local circumstances;
- the agendas of the respective partners and their potential impact in achieving behaviour change.

Settings

Initiatives are likely to be most cost-effective if based in a specific setting or settings which already have an infrastructure and support in place. Settings provide a means of gaining access to young people as well as a location in which an initiative can take place.

Schools offer the most obvious setting for physical activity initiatives aimed at young people. However, the development of initiatives in other settings is important, to broaden the range of activity opportunities available and to encourage young people to take responsibility for their own activity in preparation for later life. Following is a brief outline of some potential settings.

Schools

Schools provide a valuable setting in which to target young people, as they have a captive audience, and as the Physical Education National Curriculum requires schools to provide physical education to all young people aged 5–16 years. Schools can also be valuable in introducing students to opportunities available in other settings.

Within the school setting there are three potential areas for promoting physical activity:

Curriculum

The National Curriculum provides a framework within which young people can acquire the skills, knowledge and understanding to engage in an active lifestyle. However, time available is often limited, restricting the range of activities that can be offered to students. Research also indicates that the activities offered in the school curriculum do not always correspond to those young people prefer to take up in their own time.

Extra-curricular time

Additional opportunities exist during break-times and after school to provide physical activity opportunities for young people. There is more flexibility as to the range and types of activity that can be offered at these times. Although such opportunities are very accessible to young people in terms of location and cost, research indicates that they tend to be dominated by competitive team sports and do not cater for all students.

Links with other settings

Establishing links between schools and other appropriate settings within the local community is vital and the need for physical education teachers to establish such links is acknowledged in the National Curriculum's non-statutory guidance. Such links will help introduce young people to the wide range of options available and will provide them with the confidence and knowledge they need to participate in physical activity independently.

Case study 13 – Active Lifestyles, Bromley

Part of the Active Lifestyles Project is a health-related fitness package designed for use with children at Key Stage 1 in primary schools. This package has been developed to encourage more children to become more active and gain a positive attitude towards physical activity. The programme is designed to encourage all children, whatever their ability, to participate in and enjoy the activities offered. Prior to taking part in the project, schools are offered the opportunity to try a free taster session. The package consists of six one-hour sessions which take place during curriculum time and are led by a qualified coach arranged by the Active Lifestyle team. These sessions contribute towards the children's physical education lessons and links are made with the Physical Education National Curriculum. *See* p. 67.

Case study 14 – Wessex Healthy Schools Award

The Wessex Healthy Schools Award is a 'standardised accreditation scheme which encourages schools to make school a health-promoting experience for all who teach, learn and work in it'. The scheme has been developed by an alliance of pilot schools representing Key Stages 1–4, together with health professionals, education inspectors and advisers. Schools assess their current situation and set appropriate targets in a range of health-related areas which have been identified by a steering group. *See* p. 68.

Case study 15 – Enhancing the quality of play in the playground

This is a joint project between West Sussex Education Department and Health Promotion West Sussex, aimed at primary school children aged 4–11 years. The project aims to support schools in enhancing the quality of play at playtime through promoting a range of physical activities which improve children's health, raise self-esteem and develop their social skills. Training is provided and participants in the training programme collect and analyse data from their own school playground to help identify priorities. *See* p. 70.

Case study 16 – Rural Recreation after-school clubs, Newbury

Newbury District Council's Rural Recreation team have been running an after-school club service for rural primary schools for over seven years. These clubs are heavily subsidised by Newbury District Council with participants also paying a nominal charge. They provide children with activity opportunities that would not otherwise be available. The initiative is run by a team of four fieldworkers and one supervisor, all of whom have a number of sports-coaching, recreation and child-care qualifications. Each project usually runs for 1–2 terms during which time an attempt is made to recruit volunteers who can continue to run the clubs after this period. *See* p. 72.

Youth clubs

Due to the lack of constraints, a wide range of options can be provided and young people can also be given opportunities to organise and lead activities. A potential problem is that many youth club leaders have little or no specialist knowledge of physical activity. Specialist workers could be invited into the youth club setting but this will have cost implications.

Case study 17 – Hi Energy, Rotherham

This project aims to provide an opportunity for young people aged 11–18 years to participate in exercise-to-music activities (e.g. street dance, aerobics, skipping, circuits) within the youth club setting. These activities are used to motivate and involve young people, and a variety of participatory learning activities are employed to look at health issues. The project has a commitment to the promotion of holistic health and aims to raise awareness of the issues related to heart health. Young Asian women and disabled young people are identified as particular target groups. *See* p. 73.

Sports clubs

There are many sports clubs and associations throughout the country which offer a potentially extensive network of activity opportunities for young people. Sports clubs are particularly relevant for young people wishing to pursue a specific activity. They provide access to coaches and leaders with expertise in the relevant sport and provide an opportunity to develop skills in a supportive environment and take part in sport in a formal structure alongside peers.

Recent research has indicated that this is one of the main settings in which young people take part in sport outside of school lessons, particularly in the case of boys. However, there is a tendency for these clubs to focus on the most able and to cater more adequately for the needs of adults rather than young people.

If young people are to be encouraged to take advantage of the opportunities offered by sports clubs, there is a need for the clubs to be more sympathetic to the specific needs of young people; and to cater for beginners as well as those who are more competent.

Improved communication between schools and sports clubs is also required to increase young people's awareness of the range of clubs available and to help them make the first step towards joining such a club.

Case study 5 – The Sports Link Scheme

As outlined earlier (*see* p. 22) this is an example of a project aimed at encouraging young people to join local sports clubs through the development of links between upper/high schools and clubs. Members of local clubs with youth sections were invited to an initial meeting to raise awareness of the proposed Sports Link Scheme. Steps taken have included the involvement of coaches from local clubs in leading after-school clubs at schools; the organisation of introductory courses for young people by clubs; and the provision of special discounted rates for young people by clubs. *See* p. 54.

Case study 18– Sports Zone, Aylesbury

Sports Zone is a project aimed at enhancing the sporting and recreation opportunities available to young people aged 8–13 years. The project currently involves three sports – archery, golf and table tennis, with trampolining being introduced as a new sport. These sports were chosen as a result of data obtained from questionnaires distributed to children through schools. Each sport was considered in detail and a development plan produced. As a result of the project, participation in existing clubs by young people has been stimulated, and a table tennis scheme to link up schools with the local club has been initiated. *See* p. 75.

Leisure centres and facilities

These provide opportunities for young people to participate in physical activity either on a formal or informal basis. Particular advantages include:

- access to attractive, quality facilities;
- a broad range of activity options and activity classes run by qualified leaders;
- the opportunity for young people to select the type of activity they enjoy and to participate with friends in an informal atmosphere;
- refreshment facilities which allow young people to socialise after physical activities.

Participation in physical activity at leisure centres and facilities by young people can be limited through:

- poor accessibility, with limited public transport available;
- dependence on parental support and transport;
- high costs;
- a lack of awareness of the opportunities available;
- inappropriate provision for young people;

- young people's lack of confidence in taking the first step to attend;
- concerns about participating alongside other more competent or fitter participants.

Case study 19 – Leisure for Life, South Hams

Leisure for Life was launched in the summer of 1994 at one of South Hams Community Colleges to help meet the aims of the existing sport and recreation strategy. An initial survey indicated that local leisure centres and associated clubs had a low number of junior members and this provided the impetus for developing a school/centre/club initiative. In the early stages the views of 'A' level students were obtained to ensure that the project evolved into one with which young people would wish to be involved. A booklet has been produced which includes details of appropriate activities available at the leisure centre and information on local clubs together with a range of discount and free session vouchers. Students in Year 11 (i.e. school leavers) are provided with free taster sessions at the local leisure centre in curriculum time. *See* p. 76.

Local community facilities

There are various advantages to the use of community facilities such as village halls, which:

- provide an accessible setting;
- enable young people to take part in physical activity with friends and peers in an informal, friendly environment;
- are often able to provide activities at a relatively low cost;
- are able to offer physical activities which are more readily structured to address the needs of local young people;
- often provide young people with the opportunity to take an active role in the organisation and provision of activities.

However, there are potential drawbacks:

- facilities and equipment tend to be limited;
- the multi-use nature of the facilities can create potential conflicts;
- a reliance on local volunteers or the recruitment of specific leaders to provide appropriate opportunities can limit the range of options available.

Case study 20 – Kids EXCEL, Sefton

Kids EXCEL (Enjoy Xercise Create Enhanced Lifestyle) is based on a health alliance between Sefton Health and Sefton Leisure Services Department with an Exercise and Health Development Officer managing the initiative. It provides the opportunity for young people aged 8–12 years to increase their levels of activity in a fun-orientated, non-competitive way. Activities are offered in a variety of venues including church halls, town halls, sports centres and schools. The scheme provides access to a wide variety of activities including health-related games, aerobics or step for children, sports-specific sessions and parachute-canopy fun. In addition, a learning element on heart health is included to encourage children to understand the benefits of regular exercise participation and the link with maintaining good health. Every child has the opportunity to experience success on the associated Passport to Health and Fitness, a participation award scheme. *See* p. 78.

Case study 21 – Dance for Life, Bradford and Keighley

Dance for Life is a project targeted at young people aged 9–18 years, in particular girls aged 13–15 years and Asian girls. The project is based in areas of high deprivation and high incidence of coronary heart disease, and a large percentage of young people from black and ethnic minorities are involved as participants. Dance for Life aims to encourage young people regardless of age, sex, ability or ethnic origin, to dance and to develop positive attitudes to health. Sessions provide young people with a variety of dance experiences that develop skills and encourage regular participation in physical activity. The project operates in a variety of settings including community centres, sports and recreation centres and schools (both in the curriculum and extended curriculum). Other features of the project include an annual summer school for more able students and inset training for teachers to encourage dance in schools. *See* p. 80.

Parks, playgrounds and the countryside

They provide opportunities for young people to participate in a wide range of physical activities either informally or as part of an appropriate club or group. Generally, they do not charge for the use of facilities, and can be used at any time of the day by people of all ages. They are found in most localities and are accessible to the majority of young people.

However, parental concerns over their children visiting such places without supervision restrict the extent to which young people can take advantage of these opportunities.

Case study 22 – Family Fun Trail – Barnsley
The Family Fun Trail was set up in Barnsley's Dearne Valley Park to enable and encourage more people to be more active, more often. The trail is targeted at family groups, toddlers and young people aged 5–14 years. Staff from Health Promotion and the Countryside section of Barnsley Metropolitan District Council formed the initial working group with representatives from South Yorkshire Orienteering providing help with the design of the trail and the production of an accompanying map. The Trail comprises a series of twelve wooden marker posts set out around the park and connected by a number of footpaths. Using the map for guidance, participants are encouraged to find each of the markers and collect relevant information that is displayed on plastic disks, with a range of different symbols and tasks to cater for different ages. Answer sheets can be entered into a draw for a free T-shirt. Exploratory work was carried out with children from local nursery and primary schools to ensure the suitability of the designs for the markers. *See* p. 82.

Case study 23 – Trekkers, East Sussex
The Trekkers project, targeted at special needs groups of all ages, is based in Seven Sisters Country Park in Seaford, East Sussex. A family-centred cycling centre has been set up at the park, with specially adapted bicycles available for those with special needs. Special needs schools were involved in the development of the initiative and the centre is attended by a number of special needs schools on a regular basis. *See* p. 83.

Target groups

Before interventions can be developed the specific group to be targeted needs to be identified. A target group of young people incorporates a wide cross-section of individuals, and some may prefer to identify a more specific target group defined by such criteria as:

- age range;
- gender;
- ethnic group;
- activity status;
- special characteristics;
- socio-economic group;
- geographical locality in which individuals live;
- a combination of these.

Trying to address the needs of all young people in an area with one initiative may be inappropriate and impractical; although no target group will be homogenous, it is easier to address the needs of smaller target groups selected on the basis of specific criteria. The information collected by a needs analysis and audit will help to highlight priorities, and if sufficient resources are available, a range of initiatives could be developed to target different groups.

- The St Edmundsbury Leisure Development Initiative (*see* pp. 19 and 53) encompasses four projects, each aimed at a different age range, which collectively target all young people aged 1–18 years.

- Projects such as the Coventry Young People and Sport Programme (Case study 24) have identified all young people as the target group (i.e. those aged 0–21 years).

- Many projects are based on target groups of a specific age range, e.g. the Rompers scheme (Case study 25) targets pre-schoolers; the Active Lifestyles Project (Case study 13) targets children of primary school age; and the Sports Link Project (Case study 5) focuses on young people aged 14–18 years.

- Some initiatives have also used other criteria to more clearly identify their target group, e.g. the Dance for Life project (Case study 21) targets young people aged 9–18 years, with a particular focus on girls aged 13–15 years and Asian girls. The health and exercise club initiative in Somerset (Case study 4) targets young people aged 14–16 years of mixed sex who are low participants and live in rural areas.

Appropriate interventions

In order to be most effective, interventions should:

- **Address the specific needs of the young people targeted:** The information from a needs analysis and audit should help identify these needs, taking into account the preferences and priorities of the young people targeted; factors such as accessibility and the existence of support structures which influence their ability to participate. The involvement of young people themselves in the planning and development of an initiative will also help to ensure that the final project is relevant and attractive. (*See* Case study 19.)

- **Take account of young people's stage of change in relation to physical activity:** It is thought that people will go through stages of change related to physical activity. It is important to establish which stage the target group is at and target the intervention at moving them towards the next stage. Table 2 (p. 36) shows an outline of the stages in behaviour change in relation to physical activity.

  It is important to recognise that the type of initiative that is appropriate at each stage will depend on the age of the young people being targeted and their specific needs. For example, focusing on the long-term health benefits of physical activity, such as a reduction in coronary heart disease, may not be appropriate for primary school children.

Table 2 Stages in physical activity behaviour change related to young people

	Stage 1	Stage 2	Stage 3	Stage 4	Stage 5
Characteristics of the stage	Awareness of the problem of inactivity and its consequences.	Acknowledgement of the need to take part in more physical activity.	Consideration of the costs and benefits of participating in physical activity.	Start to take part in more physical activity.	Continue with more active lifestyle.
Needs at this stage	Information on inactivity and its potential impact on young people's short- and long-term health.	Opportunities to help each young person appreciate that this issue is important for them.	Opportunities for young people to discuss the pros and cons of participating in physical activity.	Providing young people with knowledge of local facilities and activity opportunities and giving them cues for action.	Establishment of a support structure to enable young people to continue participating in physical activity.
Example of an appropriate initiative	*Keep Fit and Hearty Pack* (Case study 26) to help children understand the relationship between physical activity and health and provide advice on safely participating in physical activity.	*Mobile Fitness Factor* (Case study 27) Assembly and activity day for children to try activities and learn about the effects of exercise. *Bodycare Roadshow* (Case study 3) Individual fitness assessments together with supporting information.	*Exercise Roadshow* (Case study 28) Roadshow highlights benefits of activity and illustrates accessible forms of activity. Provides opportunity for discussion of the relevant issues.	*Leisure for Life* (Case study 19) Young people provided with booklet summarising available physical activity opportunities in the local community and given free sessions in curriculum time to try out some of these.	*Coventry Sport and Young People Programme* (Case study 24) Provides support for delivery of PE in schools; development and delivery of after-school sports opportunities; and work with clubs to make them more appropriate for participation by young people.

- **Take account of current physical activity recommendations for young people:** Although there are no firm national guidelines in this area it is important to take current recommendations into account (*see* page 9).

- **Provide physical activity opportunities of a high standard:** Young people have unique physical characteristics and needs. It is important that the activity leaders involved in delivering initiatives are aware of these factors and that they are appropriately qualified. Relevant in-service training may be appropriate (*See* Case study 9).

- **Be part of a longer-term programme:** Whilst a one-off, high profile promotion can be effective to raise the profile of physical activity and motivate young people to be more active, this in itself is unlikely to be effective in stimulating actual behaviour change unless accompanied by a programme providing long-term support and provision.

Case study 27 – The Mobile Fitness Factor, Dudley

The Mobile Fitness Factor is concerned with increasing the activity levels of young people aged 7–18 years. Two initiatives have been developed, one for 7–11-year-olds and the other for 11–18-year-olds, both of which are school-based. The project for those aged 7–11 years highlights how a initial event can be followed up by supportive follow-on developments. A play is presented in a school assembly in which children are introduced to 'Deano the Dinosaur' and the Fitlife plan. Deano is a fun character used to promote the scheme and appears on all literature and leaflets associated with the Fitlife plan. An activity day aims to motivate children to become more active. During this day children take part in a circuit-based activity which teaches them about the effects of this activity on their bodies. The assembly and activity day help to motivate children to take part in the Fitlife plan over the following four weeks. Each child receives a Fitlife plan which encourages them to participate in physical activity and eat healthy foods. Goals are set in each of these areas for the following four weeks and children record their progress by colouring in sections in their Fitlife Plan leaflet. On completion of the one-month period, Deano the Dinosaur returns to the school and each child who has completed the Fitlife plan receives a certificate. See p. 88.

- **Be designed to be sustainable and provide continued long-term support:** Interventions aimed at providing improved provision and support for young people which will continue in the long term are likely to have the most overall impact. Most initiatives are based on specific periods of funding. There is a need to develop interventions that can be sustained beyond this funding period.

Case study 4 – Health and exercise clubs for young people, Mendip District

Ensuring continued provision is identified as an important aspect of this project. The aim is to give young people the responsibility for organising activities within a given framework and sustaining the provision after the project has moved on. Training opportunities are to be provided for participants and/or local leaders to enable them to ultimately organise independent village activity. Courses providing advice on fund-raising, group organisation, and awareness of other facilities, groups and organisations with which links can be established. *See* p. 53.

Physical activity may be promoted to young people either directly or indirectly. Direct interventions could include the provision of specific activity clubs or sessions as illustrated by the Arun Holiday activities (Case study 6). The introduction of traffic calming measures, as included within the Sustrans Healthy Routes to Schools initiative (Case study 8), or the development of more safe play areas are examples of indirect interventions.

Costs and resourcing

An implementation plan needs to include a clear breakdown of the anticipated costs. These may include:

- staffing costs (either direct or indirect);
- office costs;
- resourcing costs.

It is important to take into consideration the potential funds that are available; interventions involving more than one partner are likely to have access to more financial resources.

A distinction needs to be made between initial set-up costs and those costs which are ongoing. Funding is often available on a short-term basis, therefore it is important that interventions are developed that can be sustained with little or no further costs after the end of the funding period. (*See* Case study 22).

Training needs

It is important to identify any training which is needed to underpin a project. Training helps to ensure that delivery is of a high standard and that those involved are appropriately qualified. Training also helps to create a valuable pool of leaders who can help to support and sustain the promotion of physical activity.

In assessing training needs, it is important to consider general training needs (related to promoting physical activity to young people); and specific training needs (related to the implementation of a specific initiative).

Quality training is particularly important:

- if interventions involve leaders who have no prior knowledge or expertise in promoting physical activity to young people;
- for interventions which operate across a range of settings, to provide individuals with a better understanding of the work of their colleagues in other settings, e.g. school-based interventions involving an input from outside agencies may incorporate training to ensure that educational objectives are maintained.

(For details of existing training opportunities organised by national agencies see p. 103, Appendix 3. Various local agencies also organise training opportunities, and their details are listed in Appendix 2, p. 100)

The Exercise Roadshow (Case study 28) and Hampshire Physical Education and Sport Partnership (Case study 9) are both underpinned by training, and training forms a central element of the Get Active Programme and the Youth Sports Development Project, Gloucestershire.

> ### Case study 29 – The Get Active Programme
> The Get Active Programme aims to improve the health and fitness of individuals with learning disabilities and to help them develop a sufficient level of fitness to enable participation in other activities. An extensive resource pack has been developed to help carers, Gateway Club leaders, leisure service providers, health and fitness service providers and other interested people to safely and effectively promote physical fitness among the target group. A comprehensive training course has been developed for all those wishing to utilise these resource materials and as a consequence a human resource pool of knowledgeable, confident tutors is being created with the resources to effect change. *See* p. 91.
>
> ### Case study 30 – The Youth Sports Development Project, Gloucestershire
> The Youth Sports Development Project aims to provide, promote and develop good quality sports opportunities for young people in Gloucestershire aged 11–25 years, particularly young people within the youth service. Relevant training is being provided to help increase the quality of sports leadership and coaching available to young people. A central aspect of this project has been the setting up of a full programme of sports training courses for youth workers and students from the local college. Courses provided include the Community Sports Leader Award, National Coaching Foundation courses and National Governing Body courses. *See* p. 93.

Responsibilities and co-ordination

A number of elements are important to facilitate the effective implementation of an intervention:

- identify a clear management structure;

- provide a clear indication of the relevant responsibilities of all those involved. This is particularly important if an initiative is being co-ordinated by a partnership of key agencies;

- nominate an overall co-ordinator and/or lead agency;

- ensure that the designated co-ordinator or lead agency takes into account the range of priorities and agendas of all of the organisations involved in an initiative;

- develop a common framework within which all of the participating organisations can operate to achieve the common aim of increased levels of physical activity among young people.

The Hampshire Physical Education and Sport Partnership (Case study 9) clearly identifies the relative responsibilities of those involved in the project, as illustrated in Figure 2. A newly developed Education/Community steering group is responsible for policy decisions and an implementation group is responsible for putting these policies into practice.

Figure 2: Management Structure of the Hampshire Physical Education and Sports Partnership (Case study 9)

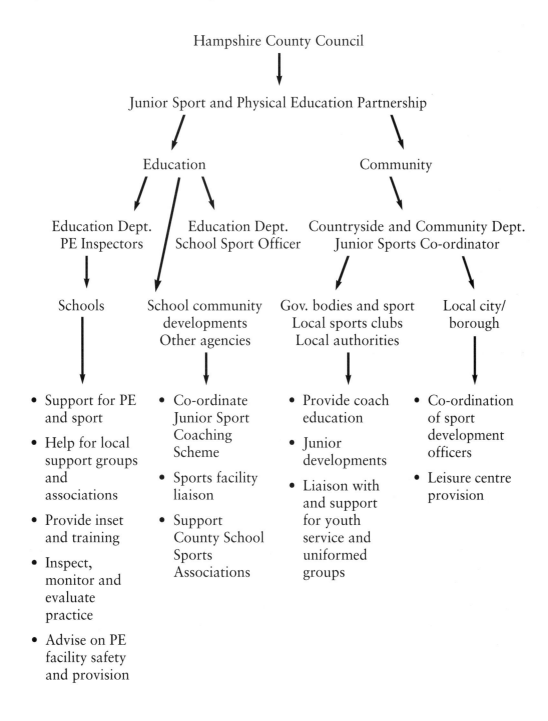

The most effective method of publicity

Effective publicity is crucial to the success of initiatives aimed at promoting physical activity to young people. Schemes aimed at increasing awareness of the benefits of physical activity or of the availability of physical activity opportunities are particularly reliant on effective communication. Some of the main methods of publicity include:

Direct contact

Visits to talk to young people about an initiative and introduce relevant personnel can help to increase awareness and also to allay some of the fears young people have about taking the first step to participate in an activity. Settings such as schools and youth clubs provide an ideal place to do this.

Promotional events

Promotional events such as activity days and taster sessions can be useful to increase awareness about physical activity in general and about specific opportunities.

Posters, leaflets, booklets

Such materials provide a relatively easy way of reaching large numbers of young people and can be useful to raise awareness, provide information and reinforce messages. In order for them to be as effective as possible, materials:

- should be displayed and distributed in relevant settings such as schools, youth clubs, village halls, community centres, libraries and sports/leisure centres;
- need to be attractive to young people;
- should provide all the relevant information;
- should be pre-tested.

However, this form of publicity may not be sufficient to stimulate actual behaviour change unless combined with other approaches.

Broadcasting at a local level

Publicising initiatives on local television or radio or in local newspapers can be a useful way of promoting physical activity initiatives. Such promotions could be targeted either at the young people themselves or at parents/guardians, who have an important role to play in encouraging and supporting their children to become more active.

In order to maximise the number of young people reached it is important to consider the content of such publicity, its timing and placement.

Relying solely on mass media may not effectively achieve behaviour change among young people.

Summary

A combination of the above methods will be the most effective in making young people aware of an initiative and promoting actual behaviour change. For example the Kids EXCEL project (Case study 20) produces leaflets and posters which are distributed through schools. Demonstration sessions are held in school physical education lessons and these are thought to be the most efficient method of attracting children onto the scheme. Special events with celebrity sports guests, and press releases in the local media also help to raise the profile of the scheme.

Identifying performance indicators

As part of the implementation plan it is important to identify a range of performance indicators that can be used to measure the effectiveness of an initiative. These could include:

- changes in young people's physical activity behaviour (this is difficult as there is no single validated method);
- changes in the number and quality of physical activity opportunities for young people;
- the number of young people taking part in the new physical activity opportunities;
- measures of change in knowledge, attitudes and beliefs relating to physical activity;
- physiological measures such as resting heart rate.

These performance indicators will help in monitoring and reviewing initiatives.

STEP 6. MONITORING AND REVIEW

It is very important to constantly monitor initiatives in order to identify potential problems early on and to ensure that aims and objectives are being met.

A small number of performance indicators should be selected to provide the focus for the monitoring of a project. Data gathered could include information on:

- the quantity and quality of physical activity opportunities being offered for young people;
- the young people to whom these opportunities are being offered;
- young people's level of satisfaction with the provision.

Monitoring also helps to highlight whether or not an initiative is in line with the agreed timescale of the project. Methods of monitoring an initiative could include observation, feedback from young people and examination of relevant records.

A review should also be carried out at a specific stage in any contract period. This can provide new information on the needs of the young people being targeted which can be used to adapt the subsequent stages of the initiative.

The data from a review can help to indicate:

- how well an initiative is being carried out;
- whether the service being provided is still the most relevant for meeting the activity needs of the target group;
- whether there is a need for the initiative to be expanded or contracted;
- whether there is a need for the service to be redesigned to more effectively match resources.

All of the above information will help inform decisions about the future of the initiative and the potential for further developments.

Part of the review process may involve carrying out an initial pilot phase of an initiative on a reduced scale. Information gained from such a pilot study can be valuable in identifying potential improvements before the initiative is formally launched and before too much expense has been incurred. Pilot studies can help to highlight the value of an initiative and may provide evidence of a need for additional funding. Examples of initiatives which have carried out pilot projects include Kids EXCEL (Case study 20), Sports Link Suffolk (Case study 5) and Rompers (Case study 25).

Case study 28 – The Exercise Roadshow, Sunderland

The project uses regular monitoring to ensure it is relevant and effective. During the roadshows, the young people participating are asked for feedback, in particular whether they have any criticisms or suggestions. In addition, children's thinking and understanding of physical activity is monitored. All of the information gathered from this monitoring process is used to modify the ongoing programme. *See p. 90.*

Case study 6 – Holiday activities, Arun West Sussex

Both the young people and their parents are asked for feedback as part of the monitoring process for this initiative. The focus of the questionnaire for young people is their level of enjoyment and the identification of ways in which this could be improved, including particular activities they would like to see incorporated. The parent's questionnaire includes questions on whether or not they consider the activities offered value for money and whether they found the booking procedures satisfactory. *See p. 55.*

Feedback questionnaires are also used by the Rompers project (Case study 25), where parents are asked to comment on a range of aspects including the suitability of the venue, quality of instruction and ideas for possible improvements.

STEP 7. EVALUATION

Evaluation is an essential element of any initiative, and specific allocation should be made within a budget for this. Decisions regarding the aspects that are to be evaluated and how the evaluation is to be carried out should be made at the planning stage, and this process can help to clarify what outcomes are expected from the project. The identification of clear objectives and specific criteria by which an initiative's performance will be assessed will make the evaluation task more easy.

Evaluation procedures can collect information using a range of measures. The performance indicators outlined earlier (*see* p. 43) are particularly relevant. Evaluations help to indicate whether:

- an initiative has been effective in meeting the specified aims and objectives, and if not, why this is the case;
- the initiative has had a worthwhile impact;
- resources were used effectively;
- there are additional needs still to be addressed;
- there are any additional benefits not anticipated when the initiative was developed.

The evaluation process could be carried out by the organisations involved in managing the initiative or by an independent agent, such as a local university or college. It is important that the methods used for evaluation are reliable and valid and are appropriate for use with young people. Utilising independent evaluators with specialist knowledge and expertise can be helpful in this respect. For example, monitoring and evaluation for the pilot stage of the Kids EXCEL project (Case study 20) was carried out by Liverpool John Moores University.

Information gained from an evaluation is also valuable in highlighting priorities for future work. Data collected from evaluations should be disseminated through reports and workshops.

The Leisure for Life project (Case study 19) used a number of indicators to evaluate the project. Below is an outline of the stated aims of the project and how they were evaluated:

Stated aim	Evaluation procedure
To encourage greater participation in leisure centre and sport club activities by young people.	Feedback is obtained from clubs and leisure centres. A record is made of all the scheme vouchers for sports club/leisure centre activities which have been redeemed by young people.
To encourage active lifestyles among young people.	Information on the redemption of vouchers and increased participation at sports clubs/leisure centres. An evaluation form is circulated to all young people involved in the scheme. As part of this, young people are asked whether or not they intend to use the Leisure for Life booklet they have been given.
To promote good public relations with schools.	Feedback is obtained from heads of physical education departments in schools.

The evaluation form given to young people involved in the Leisure for Life project also asks for details on how informative the project has been, and suggestions for improvements. An important point made by the project is that the timing of evaluations can have an influence on results. For example, one group of girls who had participated in the Leisure for Life Project in the summer term did not actually start participating in aerobics sessions at the local leisure centre until the autumn as the girls felt it was too hot to participate in aerobics in the summer. Since the evaluation is normally undertaken immediately after completion of the project, such changes would not be recorded and the full extent of the impact of the project may not be measured.

The evaluation of other projects includes both quantitative and qualitative aspects. For example, the project promoting Health and Exercise Clubs in Mendip (Case study 4) collects information on a range of quantitative and qualitative measures.

Quantitative measures include a percentage of permanent activity established; a percentage of young people who take up physical activity on a regular basis and measured increases in fitness levels among the target group.

Qualitative measures include evidence of improved lifestyle awareness and habits; evidence of change in participation habits; and results of participant surveys incorporating quality of life perceptions and responses to the service offered (including future suggestions).

The availability of initial baseline data can help to highlight changes promoted by an initiative. For example, a previous study which monitored levels of physical activity for school children within Sefton has been used as a baseline for comparing the effects of the Kids EXCEL (Case study 19) scheme on short and long term participation in exercise.

Summary

Following are six key questions to consider when designing interventions targeting young people and physical activity:

- What types of physical activity should be promoted?

- In which settings should the initiative operate?

- Should the promotion of physical activity occur throught direct or indirect means?

- Should efforts be made to influence local policies to benefit physical activity promotion?

- Is an initiative best pursued as a single event or a longer-term programme with on-going provision?

- What types of publicity and communication should be used to promote the initiative?

The case studies that follow provide a valuable starting point for those wishing to develop similar projects and interventions. They are based upon a variety of locally developed strategies to promote physical activity for young people. All the contacts listed have indicated a willingness to share their knowledge and experiences with other professionals, and are able to provide useful guidance on both the benefits and pitfalls of their unique and differing approaches.

The case studies are a detailed analysis of thirty local initiatives, preceded by a matrix providing at-a-glance information on each one.

Case studies

Matrix

No.	Case Studies	Target Group							
		Age Group					Rural areas	Parents	Ethnic groups
		3–8	8–11	11–14	14–16	16–18			
1	Young people survey and audit projects, East Berkshire			●	●		●		
2	Fitness survey, Waveney		●	●					
3	Bodycare Roadshow, St Edmundsbury		●						
4	Health and Exercise Club, Mendip				●		●		
5	Suffolk Sports Link Scheme				●	●			
6	Holiday activities, Arun West Sussex			●	●				
7	Health-related exercise, Swindon								
8	Sustrans safe routes to schools		●	●	●	●			
9	Active Partners project and Hampshire PE Sport Partnership				●	●			
10	Pro-Sport								
11	Take Part in Herts	●	●	●	●	●			
12	Ready, Teddy Go, Manchester	●	●					●	
13	Active lifestyles, Bromley	●	●					●	
14	Healthy Schools Award, Wessex	●	●	●	●	●			
15	Play in the playground, West Sussex	●	●					●	
16	After-School Clubs, Newbury	●	●			●			
17	Hi Energy, Rotherham			●	●	●			●
18	Sports Zone, Aylesbury		●	●					
19	Leisure for Life, South Hams					●			
20	Kids EXCEL, Sefton		●	●					
21	Dance for Life, Bradford and Keighley		●	●	●	●			●
22	Family Fun Trail, Barnsley	●	●	●				●	
23	Trekkers, East Sussex								
24	Coventry Young People and Sport	●	●	●	●	●			
25	Rompers, St Edmundsbury	●						●	
26	Keep Fit and Hearty, Redditch	●	●						
27	Mobile Fitness Factor Dudley		●	●	●	●			
28	Exercise Roadshow, Sunderland		●						
29	Get Active Programme	●	●	●	●	●			
30	Youth Sports Development Project, Gloucestershire			●	●	●			

Special issues				Setting					National impact
Special needs	Diet	Lifestyle	Training	Schools Curricular	Extra-Curricular	Community	Sports centres	Countryside	
						●			
	●				●				
	●								
	●					●			
						●			
						●			
			●	●					
		●							●
			●	●	●				
●			●			●			●
				●	●	●	●		
	●				●	●			
				●	●				
				●					
			●		●				
					●				
						●			
					●	●			
				●			●		
					●	●	●		
			●	●	●	●	●		
								●	
●								●	
				●	●	●	●		
						●			
		●		●	●				
	●			●					
		●		●					
●			●						●
●			●			●			

CASE STUDY 1
YOUNG PEOPLE SURVEY AND AUDIT PROJECTS, EAST BERKSHIRE

Target group:	young people 5-21
Setting:	community
Location:	Royal Borough of Windsor and Maidenhead
Lead organisations:	Community Leisure Services Unit, Royal Borough of Windsor and Maidenhead in Partnership with the Centre for Nutrition and Health promotion, East Berkshire Community Health NHS Trust.
Timescale:	June 1994 and onwards for five years.

Contact:

Sean Kearns
Community Leisure Services Unit
Royal Borough of Windsor and Maidenhead
Recreation and Arts Unit
4th Floor
Berkshire House
Queen Street
Maidenhead
Tel: 01628 796227

Lesley Douglas
Centre for Nutrition and
Health Promotion
East Berkshire Community
Health NHS Trust
Demodra Road
Windsor SL4 3AW
Berkshire SL6 1NF
Tel: 01753 636750

Documentation: two reports *Sport for Young People* and *Young people and Physical Activity*

Background

The Community Leisure Services Unit in the Royal Borough of Windsor and Maidenhead in conjunction with the Centre for Nutrition and Health Promotion, East Berkshire Community NHS Trust, undertook an audit of provision and providers of sport for young people. In addition the two organisations collaborated on an 11-school survey of the factors affecting participation in physical activity and the perceptions and attitudes of young people.

Stated aims

- To provide recommendations to all parties interested in the development of sport and the promotion of physical activity for young people.
- To identify all opportunities for young people to participate in sporting activity within East Berkshire
- To identify areas of sporting need for young people
- To target priorities for sustainable development over the next five years
- To identify key organisations who are willing to support strategic initiatives
- To identify factors affecting participation in leisure time physical activity
- To identify the perceptions and attitudes of young people towards physical activity

Methods employed

- Research identified through the requirements of the Community Leisure Services Unit
- Two surveys undertaken
    - 773 young people (aged 13, 14, 15 and 17) in 11-schools in East Berkshire
    - provision in 11 key sports for young people
- Providers identified from existing information services and face-to-face interviews conducted with key organisations in providing sport for young people
- Questionnaires produced and distributed to every relevant organisation including sports clubs, youth groups and schools.
- Summary of results compiled to illustrate common issues and priorities.
- Draft reports compiled for consultation with all related organisations prior to final report being produced

Lessons learned

Clarify end goals
Set better deadlines
Inform more organisations
Involve young people

Impact

1500 copies of report distributed
Recommendations drawn up for development of 11 individual sports
Strong focus and basis for future partnerships
Catalyst for change and influence

CASE STUDY 2
FITNESS SURVEY, WAVENEY

Target group:	children aged 8–14 years
Setting:	primary, middle and high schools
Location:	Waveney District, Suffolk
Lead organisations:	Waveney District Council
Other organisation involved:	Lowestoft College
Timescale:	May 1995 to present
Cost:	£4000 survey analysis
	other costs not yet quantified.
Source of funding:	Waveney District Council
Contact:	Graham Osborne (Principal Leisure Development Officer)
	Waveney District Council Community Services Department
	Mariners Street
	Lowestoft, Suffolk NR32 1JT
	Tel: 01502 523005

Background

The Fitness Survey:
- was inspired by the results of the Allied Dunbar National Fitness Survey;
- was carried out to obtain local information on children's fitness and lifestyle;
- was based on a similar survey carried out by St Edmundsbury Borough Council (see next case study);
- was relevant to the Sport Development programme which has children's fitness as the main theme.

Stated aims

- To establish the fitness levels of the district's children.
- To gather information on lifestyle and diet.
- To produce data for comparison with other districts and countries.

Methods employed

The Fitness Survey was carried out in 9 schools (3 primary, 3 middle, 3 high) and comprised:
- fitness testing based on Eurofit and administered by students of Lowestoft College;
- an administered questionnaire including questions on physical activity and eating habits;
- a food diary.

Data analysis was carried out by St Edmundsbury Borough Council, with further analysis by Bill Tuxworth (Field Operations Officer, Allied Dunbar Fitness Survey).

Impact

Unknown at this stage.

Lessons learned

The cooperation of schools is vital.
The process takes longer than anticipated.
Discipline in administering the survey is vital.

Possible development

Removal of the food diary, which was difficult to reconcile with food questions on the questionnaire.

Key recommendation for colleagues

Speak to others who have undertaken a similar survey to avoid duplicating work.

CASE STUDY 3
BODYCARE ROADSHOW, ST EDMUNDSBURY

Target group:	children at Key Stage 2 (8–11 years)
Settings:	primary and middle schools
Location:	St Edmundsbury Borough, Suffolk
Lead organisation:	St Edmundsbury Borough Leisure Services Department
Timescale:	September 1994 to present
Cost:	£15000 salary of Fitness Development Officer, including ongoing costs
	£ 3500 resources and equipment
	£ 2000 travel expenses
Sources of funding:	St Edmundsbury Borough Council, Suffolk Health Authority, sponsorship from Bodycare Products and local leisure facilities
Contact:	Sharon Ayres (Fitness Development Officer)
	St Edmundsbury Borough Council
	Angel Hill
	Bury St Edmunds
	Suffolk IP33 1XB
	Tel: 01284 757087
Resources:	booklets and stickers (used by children)
	charts (to record information)

Background

A fitness survey carried out in St Edmundsbury revealed that most young people in the area led a very sedentary lifestyle. A Fitness Strategy was developed with the following aims:

- to increase the levels of physical activity and cardio-respiratory fitness of young people in St Edmundsbury;
- to emphasize, both in schools and in the community, the importance of regular, vigorous exercise to health.

The Bodycare Roadshow was designed to spearhead this initiative.

Stated aims

- To encourage children at Key Stage 2 to lead healthier lifestyles.
- To link in with the National Curriculum with regard to health-related exercise.

Methods employed

The Bodycare Roadshow comprises:

- a 5-week programme in primary schools (years 3 and 4), working with each class for 1 hour per week covering modules on health-related exercise;
- a motivation scheme encouraging children to participate in activity outside of school;
- a fitness test before and after the 5-week block;
- a 1-week block in middle schools, with each class offered 1 session a day, concentrating on fitness testing, health-related exercise topics and extra-curricular opportunities at lunchtimes and after school.

Impact

- Feedback from schools has been very positive, and most wanted repeat visits.
- Approximately 70% of the children improved their results on the fitness test after the 5-week period.

Lessons learned

Targeting 36 schools in one year was too ambitious. A two year rolling programme is now to be used.

Possible development

Establishing more exit routes (clubs) for children to go to following the 5-week period of the Roadshow.

Key recommendation for colleagues

Liaise with as many other organisations as possible to help back-up and reinforce messages.

CASE STUDY 4
MOBILE HEALTH AND EXERCISE CLUB FOR RURAL MENDIP

Target group:	young people aged 14–16 years who live in rural areas
Settings:	secondary schools and village halls in rural communities
Location:	Mendip District, Somerset
Lead Organisation:	Mendip District Council
Timescale:	September 1995 to August 1998
Cost:	£ 1460 initial set-up costs
	£ 10700 ongoing costs
Source of funding:	Somerset Health Authority/Health Promotion Unit
Contact:	Hayley Whittock
	Mendip Leisure
	Mendip District Council
	Cannards Grave Road
	Shepton Mallet BA4 5BT
	Tel: 01749 343399 ext. 552
Resource:	leisure questionnaire

Background
The rural health and exercise clubs were introduced in response to national evidence that:
* young people are not participating in sufficient physical activity to accrue health benefits;
* many young people are overweight;
* there is a gap in the provision for young people living in rural areas.

Stated aims
* To establish contact with the target group through schools and carry out initial consultation on current exercise habits, fitness levels and perceived needs.
* To provide a mobile health and exercise club for this age group to help increase their activity levels.

Methods employed
* A leisure questionnaire is used to gather information on the exercise habits, fitness levels and perceived needs of the target group.
* Health and exercise clubs which incorporate aerobics and circuit-training activities, advice on diet and nutrition and general input towards a healthy lifestyle, including regular fitness testing, exercise prescription and provision.
* A non-competitive, adult approach is used.
* Liaison with schools, youth service, leisure facilities etc. helps to ensure that this scheme complements the existing servies.

Impact
It is too early on in the project to assess its impact and identify specific implications.

CASE STUDY 5
SUFFOLK SPORTS LINK SCHEME

Target group:	young people aged 14–18 years (initially)
Settings:	secondary schools and local clubs
Location:	Ipswich and county of Suffolk
Lead organisation:	Suffolk County Council
Other organisation:	Sports Council (Eastern Region)
Timescale:	1987–1989 Ipswich pilot scheme
	1991–1993 County Project
	1994–1995 Follow-up Project
Cost:	£10000 Ipswich Pilot Project
	£15820 Year 1, County Project
	£17400 Year 2, County Project
	£26800 Year 3, County Project
	£ 9000 Follow-up Project
Sources of funding:	Suffolk County Council, Sports Council (Eastern Region)
Contact:	Mrs E. Delaney (County Sports Development Officer)
	Education Office
	St Andrew House
	County Hall
	Ipswich IP4 1LJ
	Tel: 01473 583000
Resources:	Ipswich Sports Directory
	Link Badge Scheme Report
	leaflet on Suffolk Sports Link Scheme

Background

Sports Link developed from discussions between the Sports Council and the County PE Adviser.

Stated aim

To develop sporting and recreational opportunities for students at upper/high school with the specific objective of increasing participation in school, sports clubs and other community-based activities.

Methods employed

Methods have varied between localities but common themes include:
- a questionnaire to identify sporting interests and participation habits of Year 10 students;
- production of a local directory of relevant sports clubs;
- encouraging the development of links between upper/high schools and sports clubs;
- encouraging students to participate in opportunities in the community and to use available sports facilities;
- encouraging clubs to form junior sections;
- providing Sports Link noticeboards in schools to provide information for students.

Impact

A significant number of the original links are still operating and have been developed further.

Lessons learned

This is an important way of offering a wide range of opportunities to young people and of encouraging continued participation in physical activities on leaving school.
Clubs need assistance in developing coaching expertise and understanding young people.

Possible developments

Further work on encouraging clubs to participate.
More involvement from governing bodies of sport.
Development of junior clubs that have an accredited standard.
Junior clubs, developed on school sites, as satellite centres of senior clubs.

CASE STUDY 6
HOLIDAY ACTIVITIES, ARUN WEST SUSSEX

Target group:	young people aged 11–16 years
Settings:	various settings in the community
Location:	Arun District, West Sussex
Lead organisations:	Arun District Council
	West Sussex Youth Service
Timescale:	September 1995 to present
Cost:	£8000 brochure and printing costs
	salary costs for 2 officers, 5 hours per week for 9 weeks
Sources of funding:	Arun District Council, West Sussex Youth Service, advertisers (in brochure)
Contact:	Emma Lindsay, Leisure Development Officer
	Arun District Council
	Maltravers Road
	Littlehampton
	West Sussex BN17 5LF
	Tel: 01903 716133
Resources:	brochure detailing available physical activity opportunities
	free sports vouchers

Background
There is already a thriving and very successful junior holiday programme in the district known as 'Oscars', and it was decided to target older children with a similar project.

Stated aims
- To encourage the target group to participate in leisure activities.
- To initiate, co-ordinate and implement a holiday programme for 11–16-year-olds.

Methods employed
- A questionnaire was used to identify which activities the target group were interested in.
- An audit was carried out to identify existing opportunities and gaps in the existing provision
  of activities.
- A number of organisations and clubs were contacted to arrange appropriate outings and sporting activities for young people in the holidays.
- Detailed information on suitable opportunities is to be compiled in an attractive brochure and circulated to the target group with free sports vouchers.

Impact
It is too early to assess the impact of the scheme.

Lessons learned
Find out what activities young people would like to do, don't make assumptions.

Key recommendations for colleagues
Create good contacts – working with the youth service has been a great advantage.
Ensure funding is available to create a good-quality brochure.

CASE STUDY 7
MAKING SENSE OF HEALTH-RELATED EXERCISE: A GUIDE FOR PRIMARY AND SECONDARY TEACHERS, SWINDON

Target group:	primary and secondary school physical education teachers
Setting:	schools
Location:	Swindon
Lead organisation:	Swindon Health Promotion Unit
Other organisations:	Wiltshire Education Support and Training, Thamesdown Borough Council
Timescale:	1995 to present
Cost:	costs for producing guide and associated training not yet known
Sources of funding:	Lifestyle at school budget – Swindon Health Promotion Unit via East Wiltshire Health Care
Contact:	Thamesdown Borough Council Raelene Croad Swindon Health Promotion Unit 3 The Mall Swindon Wiltshire SN1 4JA Tel: 01793 481182
Resources:	Making sense of health-related exercise: a guide for teachers Swindon Schools Leisure Portfolio

Background

This initiative originated in response to:
- evidence of low levels of physical activity amongst young people;
- awareness that there was a lack of related resources in the Health Promotion Unit and in schools;
- awareness that there was a lack of skills and knowledge about health-related exercise amongst teachers.

Stated aim

The aim of the guide, accompanying resources and training is: to provide physical education teachers and health co-ordinators with useful resources, units of work, advice and information, in order to raise the profile of health-related exercise and allow it to be effectively delivered within the school curriculum.

Methods employed

- A guide has been compiled for primary and secondary school teachers which includes information on health-related exercise including recommended resources and reading, and useful addresses.
- Training is to be provided based on this, and includes an overview of the philosophy, contents and application of the recommended resources together with examples of the practical application of some of the ideas described.
- Access is provided to other relevant resources, and their use is promoted through an open evening.

Complementary developments include:
- The production of a leisure portfolio.
- Activity taster sessions and classes to be offered in schools and at leisure centres on open evenings.
- Parent and child activities to be added to programmes.
- GP referrals of 13–20-year-olds for exercise programmes as displacement for smoking.

Impact

Results of training, response to teaching pack and use of extra resources yet to be determined.

Lessons learned

It is worth investing money in buying good resources for schools, provided they are disseminated with quality training.
Information needs to be kept as concise as possible.

Possible development

The involvement of local sports development officers and local university/college physical education students to help launch resources in schools.

Key recommendations for colleagues

Establish clear objectives, proposed methods and an estimated time-scale very early on in the project.
Include other professionals in the project to provide ideas, assistance and action.
Try to get support, shared responsibility and commitment from all those involved early on in the project.
Seek advice on and preview materials before buying them.

CASE STUDY 8
SUSTRANS SAFE ROUTES TO SCHOOLS

Target group:	school children/students aged 9–18 years
Settings:	junior schools, secondary schools, sixth-form colleges
Location:	York, Colchester, South-East Hampshire, Leeds
Lead organisation:	Sustrans
Other organisations:	City of York Council, Colchester Borough Council, Hampshire County Council and Leeds City Council
Timescale:	autumn 1995 to autumn/winter 1998
Cost:	£40000 administration and project management
	£ 5000 educational material
	£ 5000 research/analysis
	£10000 technical design
Sources of funding:	Department of Environment – Environmental Action Fund, local authority highways budgets, anonymous trusts, schools and Sustrans
Contact:	Paul Osborne
	16 Wilton Rise
	York YO2 4BW
	Tel: 01904 651506
Resource:	Safe Routes to Schools Information Sheet, teacher information folder, newsletter, video
Special features:	promotes physical activity built into daily life

Background
- Safe routes to schools projects were first started in the mid-eighties in Manchester and Bristol.
- This project was developed as the first comprehensive safe routes to schools project taking place across the country.

Stated aims
- To improve the levels of health and fitness of children in pilot schools.
- To reduce trips to and from school by car, and thereby reduce pollution and congestion.
- To improve safety and reduce accident numbers and severity.

Methods employed
- Before-study questionnaires were administered and the results used to analyse travel patterns, areas for potential danger reduction, current activity levels.
- In consultation with children, staff and parents, appropriate measures were identified to encourage walking and cycling to school and in leisure time. These included traffic calming, cycle paths, safe crossings, bicycle sheds, health promotion education, awareness raising.
- Proposals were costed and detailed designs submitted for measures to be implemented over 3 years.
- After-study questionnaire was administered to identify changes from baseline.

Impact
Results of after-study questionnaire not yet available.

Lessons learned
It is difficult to measure changes in health and fitness of adolescents because of corresponding physical changes as they mature. It is more useful to measure changes in the frequency or type of activity.
It is difficult to assess how much this project has contributed towards improved health and fitness.

Possible development
There is need for more flexibility in handling cross-sectional budgets i.e. more cycling (generally paid for out of Highways budgets) can generate savings in school bus costs (Education budgets) and health savings.

CASE STUDY 9
THE ACTIVE PARTNERS PROJECT AND HAMPSHIRE PHYSICAL EDUCATION SPORT PARTNERSHIP

Target group:	students of school age (4–16) and young people aged 16–18
Settings:	schools (curricular and extra-curricular) and community
Location:	County of Hampshire
Lead organisations:	Education Department PE Inspectors
	Sports Council Southern Region Officers
Other organisations involved:	Hampshire Inspectors Advice and Support Services, Hampshire Education Department Countryside and Community Department
Timescale:	1991 to present
Cost:	examples include:

£24000+   oncosts for teacher adviser years before the project
£10000+   to deliver governing body development plans
£18000   Top Play and Top Sport training and equipment

Sources of funding:	Sports Council, direct funding
	Hampshire Education Department, indirect funding
Contact:	Steve Poynton
	General Inspector Physical Education
	Hampshire Inspection, Advisory and Support Services
	Central Divisional Education Office
	Clarendon House
	Romsey Road
	Winchester, Hants. SO22 5PW
	Tel: 01962 876286
Documentation:	Active Partner Project Information Leaflet
	booklet/support documentation to initiate each new project
	Inset-related documentation relevant to each specific course
Special features:	co-ordinated county-wide project
	multi-agency approach

Background

- The project was inspired by the Active Lifestyle project in Coventry.
- A physical education conference was organised and a rationale was established with principles and ways of working.

Stated aims

The Active Partners Project
- To improve the quality of physical education in Hampshire schools and colleges.
- To promote pathways for students to increase participation in and out of school.
- To provide a structure that is a continuous and progressive experience for students, developing from the existing educational infrastructure.

The Hampshire Junior Sport and Physical Education Patrtnership
- To provide support for physical education and sport in schools by providing in-service training, monitoring practice and advising on safety and provision.
- To promote school to community developments.
- To provide support to various agencies through education and advice.
- To co-ordinate local city/borough sport development officers and provide advice on leisure centre provision.

Methods employed

- An audit was conducted to ascertain the current provision of physical education, sport and activity opportunities for young people in and out of school.
- Action plans were established and a number of relevant schemes introduced.
- Example schemes were offered and set up and all examples of good practice were promoted and disseminated.

- The early and active involvement of all relevant parties was encouraged. All groups had a significant role in making it a multi-agency project.
- Opportunities provided for young people were structured and progressive and a variety of strategies were adopted to foster increasing independence.
- Leadership opportunities were provided for young people with help and advice.
- Appropriate training was made available to all adults involved.

Impact

A firm partnership between the relevant groups is well established.

The existing projects are valuable in the intiation of further developments.

The project is frequently evaluated by teacher advisers/inspectors and the Sports Council, and numerous conference presentations have been made.

Lessons learned

It is important not to be too ambitious; to communicate with the target group and to market the product well; to develop mutual trust between the relevant partners; to work from a true rationale with established principles; and to ensure that the product is of a high quality and is monitored.

Possible developments

To attract prime movers and funding.

To market and support existing good features.

Key recommendations for colleagues

Understand your target area thoroughly.

Establish an effective management structure.

Do not rush into any developments – ensure quality not quantity.

CASE STUDY 10
PRO-SPORT

Target group:	disabled people including young people, women and girls and ethnic groups
Settings:	local authority leisure services, schools, governing bodies of sport, Sports Council (Northern Region), disability sports organisations
Location:	Northumberland, Cumbria, Durham, Tyne and Wear, Cleveland
Lead organisations:	Sports Council (Northern Region), local authorities: Gateshead, Middlesborough, Tynedale, Durham, Allerdale, Copeland, Hartlepool, Carlisle, Sedgefield
Timescale:	July 1994 to July 1997
Cost:	salary costs for 2 officer posts various costs for individual projects
Sources of funding:	Sports Council (Northern Region) meet salary costs Teeside Tertiary College, Middlesborough and Durham University, local authorities and governing bodies, Foundation for Sport and Arts, National Lottery
Contact:	Stuart Braye Pro-Sport Teeside Tertiary College Marton Campus Marton Road Middlesborough, TS4 3RX Tel: 01642 318088
Documentation:	information Sheet original work programme
Special features:	only and first sports forum of disabled people in Britain

Background

- There are very few disabled people involved in the decision-making processes of sports development and there was a desire to change this.
- There is a need to provide one single contact point for those involved with promoting sport to disabled people.
- There is a need to involve more disabled people as coaches, administrators, development officers etc. not just as participants.

Stated aims

- To set up a sport forum of disabled people.
- To set up a Young Disabled People in Sport Advisory Group.
- To set up a Disability Equality Tutors Group.
- To develop policy, initiate coach education and training.

Methods employed

- Pro-Sport provides a consultation and co-ordinating service, assisting sports agencies to take responsibility for the development of equal opportunities.
- Pro-Sport is pro-active in providing a single point of contact, ensuring the involvement of the appropriate agency or individual.
- The project facilitates a number of independent and self-sustaining structures, e.g. Regional Advisory Group, Young Disabled People in Sport Advisory Group, and Disability Equality Tutors Group.
- Pro-Sport works with partner agencies to advise on issues including planning/access, training, education, coaching and policy development with particular reference to disabled people in sport.
- Pro-Sport assists disabled sports organisations to meet their commitments and promotes the services they offer.
- Pro-Sport directs local authorities, Sports Council and governing bodies towards the Sports Forum of Disabled People for full consultation.

Impact

There is a high knowledge of disability equality issues among Pro-Sport local authorities.
The success of the Sports Forum of Disabled People will sustain the involvement of disabled people in sports development in the Northern region.
The Youth Sport Trust and National Coaching Foundation have consulted with the Sports Forum of Disabled People on national projects.

Lessons learned

Involving disabled people and disability organisations work.
Having a Pro-Sport officer who is disabled helped to add credibility to the project. One forum has now been established that covers all areas of disabled people in sport.

Possible developments

The employment of more disabled people in local authority leisure services.
More disabled people qualified as coaches, PE teachers, sports studies lecturers etc.

Key recommendations for colleagues

Being a disabled person is a qualification and disabled people should be considered as a driving force behind a project of this nature.
Contact the Pro-Sport project and its partners for guidance and help.
Consider the implications of The Disability Discrimination Act 1995 in reference to 'provision of services'.

CASE STUDY 11
TAKE PART IN HERTS

Target group:	young people 0–16 years
Settings:	schools and colleges
Location:	Hertfordshire
Lead organisation:	Hertfordshire Health Promotion Agency
Other organisations:	A range of statutory and non-statutory agencies throughout the county including sports development, local authority district councils, local sports councils, primary health care services, leisure centre mangers, physiotherapists, disability organisations and social services.
Timescale:	strategy launched April 1995
Sources of funding:	Hertfordshire Health Promotion have allocated £30,000 to the strategy for 1996/7
Contact:	Adrian Coggins
	Hertfordshire Health Promotion
	Gate House
	Fretherne Road
	Welwyn Garden City
	Hertfordshire AL8 6RD
	Tel: 01707 390865
Documentation:	Take Part in Herts document available
Special features:	multi-agency approach
	local implementation groups

Background
* Take Part in Herts is a county-wide multi-agency strategy for promoting physical activity in Hertfordshire.
* The strategy is lead by Hertfordshire Health Promotion Agency, and the work is lead by a small multi-agency working group (The Physical Activity Advisory Group, PAAG) which meets to evaluate and review the implementation of the strategy.

Stated aims
* To increase the amount and quality of physical activity taken by all sections of the community
* To increase awareness, access, information and training opportunities for physical activity
* To encourage effective working partnerships between professionals and other agencies.

Methods employed
The advisory group will:
* develop the existing strategy document to provide a framework for the groups involved in its promotion;
* assist in the formation and development of Local Implementation Groups (LIGs) and act in an advisory capacity to support their actions;
* collate and disseminate examples of good practice.

Specific recommendations for young people include the following:
* young people, parents and teachers of all subjects should be educated as to the importance of regular physical activity and encouraged to include such activities as a feature of their personal, family and school life;
* young people should be taught the skills, knowledge and competence to assess and improve their own level of physical activity and should be given the opportunities to do so;
* young people should be introduced to a range of opportunities that will promote a lifelong interest in physical activity, including those in which the whole family can participate;
* the development of appropriate and challenging adventure playgrounds should be further encouraged;
* provision for pre-school children at parent and toddler clubs, swimming and gymnastics should be encouraged;
* links with local sports and recreational clubs and facilities should be created and developed.

Impact

The strategy seeks to complement existing sport-specific provision for young people by providing more generic physical activity provision for schools.

Lessons learned

Developments must be sustainable.
Developments must address broader health issues.
Developments should fit a range of curriculum opportunities.

Key recommendations for colleagues

Actively involve teachers in all aspects of the work.
Establish a model through pilot projects that can be replicated elsewhere.

CASE STUDY 12
READY TEDDY GO, MANCHESTER

Target groups:	nursery, primary and junior school children aged 3–11 years, parents and school staff
Setting:	primary and junior schools
Location:	Manchester
Lead organisation:	Manchester Health Promotion Specialist Service
Other organisations:	Mancunian Community Health NHS Trust; Sports Co-ordinator, Manchester Education Service; Leisure Services, Manchester City Council
Timescale:	1993 to 1994 pilot
	1994 to present project implemented in some schools in Manchester
Cost:	Not yet quantified. Includes training for parents, specialist coaching, running C.C.P.R. Community Sports Leaders Award, setting up tuck shop
Contact:	Vanessa Brown
	Manchester Health Promotion Service
	Withington Hospital
	Nell Lane
	Manchester M20 2LR
	Tel: 0161 291 3641
Documentation:	pack with photocopiable materials
Special features:	involvement of a range of organisations and groups

Background

- Existing research indicates low levels of activity in young people, and diets high in fats and sugar.
- A worker was appointed to develop activity and exercise amongst children in the school setting.
- It was recognised that schools as a setting have facilities and community contacts and are a point of reference for the community.
- There was a recognised need to run activities to develop positive attitudes to physical activity.
- The value of involving parents as role models for children to follow was recognised.
- Recognition of the value of healthy food choices.

Stated aims

- To develop a strategy for promoting activity and exercise amongst primary and junior school children in the school setting.
- To develop cardiovascular fitness, skills and co-ordination.
- To establish additional health-related activities in the school.
- To establish a whole school approach to food and health.

Methods employed

- Meetings were held with school staff and sports development to sound out ideas.
- After-school activity sessions for children were provided by local coaches and leaders. These were non-competitive and were based on a circuit of different exercises designed to promote cardiovascular fitness, co-ordination and skills.
- Children are encouraged to complete activity and food diaries.
- Activity sessions including exercises to music and circuits were provided for adults after school.
- Children were provided with information on physical activity opportunities in the local community.
- Links were made with the local park who provided suitable additional physical activities.
- Parents were involved in running a tuck shop in liaison with the Community Dietitian.
- Parents and other local volunteers are encouarged to take the C.C.P.R. Community Sports Leaders Award to continue providing opportunities.

Impact

Involvement of up to 40 children in the activity sessions.
70 families accessing activities in the local park.
Tuck shops selling healthier food were set up.
Positive statements from children about the value of activity and the benefits they have experienced.
The involvement of children previously uninterested in sport.
Evidence of children going on to join local clubs.

Lessons learned

Publicity is important.
It is helpful to inform parents that they act as role models.
Full commitment from the school and other key organisations is essential if the project is to achieve its objective.
The project needs to be part of a long-term approach to health education and health promotion in a school.
Success lies in making the project belong to the children so that they want to be part of it.
There is a need for specific organisation(s) to take responsibility for co-ordinating and organising the project and carrying out the essential 'donkey work'.

Key recommendations for colleagues

Gaining commitment from workers and head teachers is essential.
Development of alliances is valuable.

CASE STUDY 13
ACTIVE LIFESTYLES, BROMLEY

Target group:	children 5–11 years
Setting:	primary schools
Location:	London Borough of Bromley
Lead organisation:	Active Lifestyles
Timescale:	1994 to 1998 (further funding is hoped for after this period)
Cost:	£5000 per annum for sessional coaches
	£2000 per annum for equipment and other hired services
	£1000 to develop and produce the curriculum package plus salary of 1 full time development officer
Sources of funding:	Bromley Leisure and Community Services, Bromley Health, Serco, Sportsmatch
Contact:	Debra Hickman
	Sports Development Unit
	Central Library
	High Street
	Bromley, Kent BR1 1EX
	Tel: 0181 464 3333
Documentation:	mailshot leaflets sent to schools
	detailed information sheet for head teachers/PE co-ordinators

Background
- Existing evidence indicated low levels of physical activity among young people.
- It was recognised that exercise habits need to be developed early in life.

Stated aim
- To develop a co-ordinated approach to increasing levels of physical activity among children.

Methods employed
Active Lifestyles Development Officer liaises with primary school head teachers/PE co-ordinators to discuss the following opportunities.
- A curriculum health-related fitness package targeted at Key Stage 1. This is a 6-week package, preceded by a free taster session, with instruction by a fully qualified coach.
- 'Fitzone' after school clubs, taken by fully qualified instructors, targeted at 5–7 and 8–11 age groups. A free taster is provided which parents can attend. Costs of following sessions are covered by the children who attend.
- Exercise classes for teachers offered straight after school by trained instructors.

Impact
There are 10 after-school clubs currently running, catering for 176 children each week.

Lessons learned
Coaches need to consider whether their approach is appropriate for the school setting, e.g. the noise level must be contained more in schools than in leisure centres.

Possible developments
Fitzone clubs to become part of leisure centre programmes.

Key recommendations for colleagues
Co-ordinator needs to have a number of coaches who are qualified to teach health-related fitness to children.
The ratio of coach to children should be kept to a manageable level, e.g. 1:16.

CASE STUDY 14
HEALTHY SCHOOLS AWARD, WESSEX

Target group:	all young people aged 5–18 years in the Wessex region
Settings:	primary, middle, upper, secondary and special schools
Location:	Dorset, Wiltshire and Hampshire
Lead organisation:	Wessex Institute of Public Health
Other organisation:	Hampshire County Council Education Department
Timescale:	1992 pilot project
	1993 to present main project
Cost:	£5000 initial costs for production of resources
	£5000 running costs – administration and project management
Sources of funding:	South and West Regional Health Authority, registration fees from each school (£30 per school)
Contact:	Liz Rogers
	Wessex Institute of Public Health Medicine
	Highcroft
	Romsey Road
	Winchester SO22 5DH
	Tel: 01962 863511 ext: 507
Documentation:	information booklet
Special features:	co-operation between education and health authorities very high profile presentations attended by chief education officers and the Chief Executive of Health Commission

Background

- The project was inspired by the LAYH workplace charter to promote health in the workplace. This led to the idea of developing a similar framework for schools.
- The scheme was developed by an alliance of pilot schools (Key Stages 1–4), health professionals, education inspectors and advisers.
- The Wessex Healthy Schools Award was established, a 'standardised accreditation scheme which encourages schools to make school a health-promoting experience for all who teach, learn and work in it'.

Stated aim

To promote a whole-school approach to the promotion of health.

Methods employed

- Schools carried out a baseline audit with the help of a member of the project team, using key statements/questions.
- Appropriate targets were set using information from the audit, addressing key aspects in a range of health-related areas identified by a steering group. Three targets are set out of a possible nine, of which one is physical activity.
- In order to satisfy the criteria for the physical activity area schools are expected to demonstrate that:
  - there is a planned approach demonstrating continuity and progression throughout the Key Stages;
  - health and hygiene and aspects of safety are part of the entitlement for all students;
  - health-related exercise is integrated with other aspects of health;
  - suitable curricular and extended-curricular opportunities are offered to students;
  - opportunities for active lifestyles in the local community are promoted;
  - opportunities for physical activity are provided for adults who work in or regularly visit the school.
- Follow-up visits are made after one term to support and assess progress.
- Achievements are validated by the Ofsted Inspector (PE and PHSE).
- The award is presented by Health Commission and Chief Education Officer.

Impact

225 schools are involved in the scheme.
A 3-year evaluation started in 1995 to assess the effectiveness of the award in terms of the children's health-related behaviour and the structure and organisation of the school.

Lessons learned

Such an award must be supported by both health and education authorities.
A standardised approach is needed to ensure quality.
Support is needed for those who run and support the scheme.

Key recommendations for colleagues

Any award scheme needs to be developed in collaboration with schools.
It is important to be aware of the school's priorities, e.g. National Curriculum and Ofsted inspections.

CASE STUDY 15
ENHANCING THE QUALITY OF PLAY IN THE PLAYGROUND
WEST SUSSEX

Target group:	primary school children aged 4–11 years
Setting:	primary schools
Location:	West Sussex
Lead organisations:	West Sussex Education Department, Health Promotion West Sussex
Other organisations:	West Sussex County Council Advisory and Inspection Service, Freelance consultants
Timescale:	1995 to present pilot phase
Cost:	£8500 per annum health promotion adviser post (part-time)
	£1500 per annum administration
	£300 resources
	£495 research
Sources of funding:	West Sussex Health Authorities, West Sussex Education Department

Contacts:

Penny Parker	Nikki Gibbons
(Health Promotion Adviser)	(Advisory Head Teacher)
Health Promotion West Sussex	N. Eastern Professional Centre
Mid-Downs Locality Base	Furnace Drive
Butlers Green Road	Furnace Green
Haywards Heath	Crawley
West Sussex RH16 4BE	West Sussex RH10 6UB
Tel: 01444 255812	Tel: 01293 553297

Documentation: project programme
                                     session workbook

Background

- The project evolved in response to the Health of the Nation target for coronary heart disease.
- A health-related needs analysis was conducted, which confirmed that teachers were concerned about the lack of physical activity amongst children and about their levels of fitness.
- Health Promotion West Sussex liaised with Hull, Exeter and Loughborough Universities and with the British Heart Foundation and Great Ormond Street to justify establishing a health-related project with primary school children.
- This project was developed as a result of discussions between the West Sussex Health Authority and West Sussex Education Department on completion of a previous joint initiative – the implementation of the Fitness Challenge in schools.

Stated aim

To support schools in enhancing the quality of play at play-time by promoting a range of physical activities which improve children's health, raise self-esteem and develop social skills.

Methods employed

- Six half-day in-service training sessions are provided for 1 teacher and 1 non-teaching assistant in each participating school.
- Research is carried out on children's perceptions, and ongoing observation tasks are attached to each training session.
- On the basis of the data collected each school's priorities are identified and an action plan is developed to meet these priorities.
- Ideas are implemented and schools are supported by on-site consultancy offered by Health Promotion West Sussex and West Sussex Advisory and Inspection Service.

Impact

There has been 100% commitment from all primary schools in the initial pilot and this was identified as a definite concern of all the schools that have enlisted on the project.
Impact on the children is not yet known.

Possible development

Negotiation is taking place with regard to developing an NVQ Playwork qualification as part of the project for teaching ancillaries/lunch-time supervisors.

Key recommendations for colleagues

Establish that there is a need within the target group.
There is a need for commitment from key personnel.
Sufficient time, resources and funding need to be allocated to the project.

CASE STUDY 16
AFTER SCHOOL CLUBS, NEWBURY

Target group:	5–11-year-old children from rural primary schools
Setting:	rural primary schools
Location:	Newbury District
Lead organisation:	Newbury District Council's Rural Recreation Unit (within Recreation Department)
Timescale:	1987 to present
Cost:	£43,600 Rural Recreation has annual budget of £131,000 and approximately a third of their time is spent on this project.
Sources of funding:	Newbury District Council, participants charged 80p each time they attend
Contact:	Alison Goodall (Rural Recreation Supervisor) Newbury District Council Market Street Newbury, Berks RG14 5LD Tel: 01635 519385
Documentation:	letters for head teachers and parents
Special features:	offer a variety of activities including sport, physical games, drama and coaching

Background

* Rural Recreation was set up as a Sports Council initiative in 1986/87 then taken on and expanded by Newbury District Council.
* After-school clubs have always been part of the programme and are subsidised heavily by Newbury District Council.

Stated aim

To take recreation activities into the rural parts of Newbury District in order to provide opportunities for participation that would otherwise not be available.

Methods employed

* The head teacher is contacted by letter and the details of activities are arranged with them.
* A letter is sent to parents.
* One or two fieldworkers and one casual member of staff go out to the school to run sessions immediately after school, working with 5–30 children.
* All workers have a number of sports-coaching, recreation and child care qualifications.
* The programme of activities is varied and includes football, short tennis, kwick cricket, gymnastics, the Sports Council's TOP Sport and TOP Play programmes, and a Rural Recreation Fun Club.
* Projects usually run for one to two terms.
* An attempt is made to recruit volunteers who can continue to run the clubs.
* The Rural Recreation team support these volunteers and provide equipment and ideas.

Impact

On an annual basis, 25–30 after-school clubs are run at rural primary schools across the Newbury District.

Key recommendations for colleagues

Recruit volunteers at a very early stage.
Gain support locally from parents and teachers and encourage them to join in the sessions and eventually lead them.

CASE STUDY 17
HI ENERGY, ROTHERHAM

Target group:	young people aged 11–18 years (particularly young Asian women and young disabled people)
Setting:	youth clubs
Location:	Rotherham Borough
Lead organisations:	Rotherham Youth Service, Rotherham Health Authorities, Rotherham Education Department
Timescale:	April 1991 to June 1996
Cost:	£75,199 for last 2 years
Sources of funding:	Sports Council, British Heart Foundation, support in kind from Rotherham Youth Service and Department of Health Promotion (Rotherham Health Authorities)
Contact:	Lena Jones (Project Officer)
	Hi Energy Office
	Thurcroft Youth Centre
	Thurcroft Junior School
	Green Arbour Road
	Thurcroft
	Rotherham S66 9DD
	Tel: 01709 703484
Special features:	the use of dance as a specific medium for health promotion

Background

- The project was established as one of six HEA-funded projects to tackle teenage smoking and ran for 3 years on that basis.
- Rotherham Health Authorities then funded the project as part of its activities on teenage smoking.
- After a year it was agreed to place the project in the youth service, to be funded as a project to promote physical activity.

Stated aims

- To provide an opportunity for young people aged 9–18 years to participate in exercise-to-music activities.
- The project has a commitment to the promotion of holistic health and aims to raise awareness of issues related to heart health.

Methods employed

- The project uses dance, aerobics and other dynamic movement to involve and motivate young people.
- A variety of participatory learning activities are employed to look at health issues.
- Groups are established in youth centres consisting of approximately 6–12 young people. These groups often work towards a performance and spend time developing their dance or exercise skills.
- Groups run for a variety of different periods, from eight weeks to a whole school year.

Impact

The project has succeeded in increasing physical activity amongst young people.
The success of performances is an indicator of increased confidence and skills.
An interest in physical activity has been generated within Rotherham Youth Service.
There is now a trained team of experienced workers available.

Lessons learned

It is important to recruit staff with a good understanding of youth work.
It is important to be clear about the scope of the project; do not try to include everything, but rather focus on providing a specific range of activities well.

Possible development

A multi-media package to build on the artistic benefits of the project, originally used within the street dance component.

Key recommendations for colleagues

The optimum length of time for groups is one year.
Care needs to be taken in choosing workers – it is difficult to find people with an appropriate combination of skills.

CASE STUDY 18
SPORTS ZONE, AYLESBURY

Target group:	8–13-year-old children
Settings:	schools and local clubs
Location:	Buckingham and Winslow area
Lead organisation:	Aylesbury Vale District Council
Other organisations	Buckinghamshire County Council (up until December 1995), Sports Council (Southern Region)
Timescale:	April 1994 to present
Cost:	£6200
Source of funding:	Sports Council (Southern Region)
Contact:	Andrea Healy
	Aylesbury Vale District Council
	Leisure Services
	84 Walton Street
	Aylesbury, Bucks HP21 7QT
	Tel: 01296 555186
Documentation:	leaflets and posters

Background

- The Sports Council identified children and young people as one of the four main areas for the Regional Recreation Strategy 1990–93.
- Sports Council (Southern Region) staff time and finance were being directed towards encouraging long-term opportunities for all young people.
- This project was set up to extend opportunities available to young people by co-ordinating the different organisations in Aylesbury Vale.

Stated aims

- To enhance the sporting and recreation opportunities available to all young people in North Bucks.
- To provide sporting pathways for children aged 8–13 years to allow them to achieve their full potential.

Methods employed

- A questionnaire was given to children in schools in order to research the catchment area.
- The results of the survey pin-pointed four main sports for development; basketball, golf, table tennis and archery, with trampolining added later in the year.
- Each sport was considered in detail and a development plan produced.
- Developments have included the stimulation of junior participation in local clubs, links with schools and the establishment of a new club.

Impact

There has been increased participation in relevant local clubs.

Lessons learned

There is some difficulty in finding individuals to get involved with the project and continue running the sport when organisations wish to withdraw.

Possible development

The establishment of structures to enable the scheme to continue after the funding ceases.

Key recommendation for colleagues

Before the project is implemented, carry out extensive research of the area and identify individuals who could get involved with the project.

CASE STUDY 19
LEISURE FOR LIFE, SOUTH HAMS

Target group:	Year 9/11 students
Settings:	leisure and sports centres
Location:	South Hams District, Devon
Lead organisation:	South Hams Leisure Services
Other organisations:	Direct Services Organisation, South Hams Leisure Centres, local sports clubs, community colleges, Health Promotion South and West Devon
Timescale:	1994, 1995 and 1996 summer terms
Cost:	1995 – £1404 catering, coaches, leaflet for 500 students
	1996 – £2000 for 1000 participants
	Hire costs are a hidden cost met by Direct Services
	Officer costs are met by the Leisure Department
Sources of funding:	1994 South Hams Leisure Services (Sports Development)
	1995 South Hams Leisure Services (Sports Development) 50%
	South Hams Leisure Centres (D.S.O.) 50%
	1996 South Hams Leisure Services
	Health Promotion South and West Devon
	Natwest Bank
Contact:	Liz Slater
	Assistant Leisure Services Manager
	South Hams District Council Leisure Services
	Follaton House
	Plymouth Road
	Totnes, Devon TQ9 5NE
	Tel: 01803 861234 ext. 379
Documentation:	*Leisure for Life* booklet providing information on recreational opportunities
	poster press releases
Special features:	the involvement of young people in the decision-making process

Background

- Many clubs wanted help in attracting new junior members.
- A survey was undertaken which revealed that leisure centres had a low number of junior members.
- The results of the survey were used as a basis to set about finding a school/centre/club initiative.

Stated aims

- To encourage greater participation in leisure centre and sports club activities by young people.
- To encourage active lifestyles.
- To promote good public relations with schools.
- To meet the aims set out in the existing Sport and Recreation Strategy.

Methods employed

- The idea was developed for a leisure centre/club school initiative.
- 'A' level PE students were involved in the project to finalise the programme, name the project and design the booklet.
- Curricular time is used to give students taster sessions at the local sports centre, with an introduction to the centre by centre staff.
- Students are provided with a *Leisure for Life* booklet providing information on a variety of recreational opportunities. Free vouchers are provided for participation in certain activities at the leisure centres.

Impact

Many of the vouchers provided have been redeemed.
Pupils have started participating in new activities at the leisure centres.
Centres have been proactive in changing programmes to meet the needs of young people.

Lessons learned

Working directly with young people ensured that the programme had appeal for that age group.
The project may not have been such a success if leisure professionals had made all the decisions.
Support of clubs through the South Hams Sports Council has been important, as has the co-operation of schools and centre managers.
It is important to include a variety of exciting activities and involve sporting personalities to motivate young people.
A key to success is running it during curriculum time.

Possible developments

Sponsorship is crucial for the future of the project.
Greater links are likely to be established with Health Promotion for the 1996 project.

Key recommendation for colleagues

It is important to work with relevant partners from the outset, including schools, clubs, students, leisure and sports centres and sponsors.

CASE STUDY 20
KIDS EXCEL, SEFTON

Target group:	children aged 8–12 years who would not normally participate in exercise/sport
Settings:	schools, local authority sports centres, community halls, private sports clubs
Location:	throughout Sefton MBC, specific concentration around the Bootle Maritime City Challenge area (low socio-economic environment)
Lead organisation:	Sefton Leisure Department – Sport and Recreation Section
Other organisation involved:	Sefton Health
Timescale:	January 1995 to April 1995 pilot
	April 1995 to 1999 main scheme
Sources of funding:	Sefton Health, Sefton Leisure Services, Health Education Authority, Sponsorship (to be confirmed)
Contact:	Suzanne Roche
	Exercise and Health Development Officer
	Pavilion Buildings
	99–105 Lord Street
	Southport PR8 1RJ
	Tel: 0151 934 2355
Documentation:	promotional materials
	Passport to Health and Fitness
Special features:	Passport to Health and Fitness has been designed on a non-competitive basis
	regular displays and workshops are available for the children and instructors
	special events/promotions are made with celebrity sports guests

Background

- EXCEL (Enjoy Xercise Create Enhanced Lifestyle) is the Exercise and Health Project for Sefton, of which Kids EXCEL is the first scheme to be developed.
- Existing research evidence highlighting low levels of activity among young people prompted the decision to start with the younger age group.
- The aim of the scheme is to encourage long-term participation in exercise.
- Schemes include Exercise on Prescription, mobile fitness testing and health screening, and taster exercise schemes.
- The project has been developed through a health alliance partnership between Sefton Health and Sefton Leisure Services Department, and is in line with the Health of the Nation.
- Implementation of these schemes will be made possible through various working partnerships.

Stated aims

- To provide the opportunity for the children of Sefton to increase levels of physical activity, and improve health, through a fun-orientated, non-competitive, low-cost scheme.
- To encourage children to understand the benefits of regular exercise in maintaining good health.
- To develop a scheme which could be adopted by schools for the future.
- To monitor the short- and long-term effects of participation in the scheme for children in Sefton.

Methods employed

- Kids EXCEL provides access to a wide variety of activities, including health-related games and activities, aerobics and step for children, sports-specific guest speakers and practical sessions, parachute-canopy fun and the British Heart Foundation Jump Rope for Heart Scheme.
- A learning element on heart health aims to encourage an understanding of the benefits of regular exercise.

- Sessions are offered in a range of settings with children charged £1.00 per session.
- Activities are promoted in a fun-orientated, non-competitive way.
- A participation award initiative, 'Passport to Health and Fitness', awards points for attendance at Kids EXCEL sessions and offers a range of prizes for accumulated points.

Impact

Attendances range from 15 to 55 per session with a total of 10 sessions per week running throughout Sefton.
A high proportion of participants did not previously participate in physical activity outside of school.

Lessons learned

Distributing leaflets through schools is not an efficient method of promotion; demonstration sessions during PE lessons is more effective.
The majority of children enjoyed the small competitive element which has been introduced recently.
The Passport to Health and Fitness has provided a major incentive for children to adhere to the scheme.
An independent relationship with each school needs to be developed.
The appointment and training of instructors and the preparation of promotional material is extremely time-consuming and should be planned well in advance.
The use of the latest chart music enhances the sessions and provides the ideal learning tool for specific activities such as co-ordination and step development in skipping and circuits.

Possible developments

Appointment of an assistant to take responsibility for general administration and other tasks.
The major part of the expenditure needs to be offset through income generated, so increased attendance is a priority.
There is a great demand to develop the schemes to include those aged under eight years and 16–24 years.
An instructor training course (NVQ validated) is now being compiled with an additional day for teachers.
It is hoped the scheme will be incorporated as an extra-curricular activity by primary schools.

CASE STUDY 21
DANCE FOR LIFE, BRADFORD AND KEIGHLEY

Target group:	young people aged 9–18 years, particularly girls aged 13–15 years and Asian girls.
Settings:	schools, youth clubs, community centres, sports and recreation centres and occasionally public places such as theatres for courses or performances
Location:	Bradford and Keighley
Lead organisation:	Bradford Council
Timescale:	1992 to April 1998
Cost:	£23,970 Year 1
	£24,510 Year 2
	£26,160 Year 3
Sources of funding:	Bradford Council, Heartsmart, Foundation for Sport and the Arts,
	Yorkshire and Humberside Arts
Contact:	Cathy Middleton, Dance Development Officer
	Ground Floor
	Jacobs Well
	Bradford BD1 5RW
	Tel: 01274 75262
Documentation:	annual reports
	publicity leaflet
Special features:	mainly community based in areas of deprivation and high incidence of coronary heart disease.
	a high percentage of ethnic minorities involved as participants

Background

A combination of three factors led to the Dance for Life project being set up:
* the Heartsmart Strategy group wanted to set up a disease prevention scheme for young people;
* existing research indicates low levels of physical activity amongst young people, particularly girls;
* existing research shows that girls are more interested in dance than sports.

Stated aims

* To encourage young people, regardless of age, sex, ability or ethnic origin, to dance and to develop positive attitudes to health.
* To develop skills and encourage regular participation in physical activity.
* To acquire funding to continue the project.

Methods employed

* Half-term or termly projects were set up in curriculum time.
* After-school or lunch-time clubs were set up in the same schools.
* Sessions were set up for women and girls (including some mothers with children), in community centres.
* High-profile projects were developed, with an end point involving other artists.
* Annual summer schools were run for the more able students to train to a high level, with performances given at a central venue.
* Inset training was provided for teachers to encourage dance in schools, and training was provided for dance workers.

Impact

There have been nearly 5000 participants since 1992.
Regular participation and enjoyment are viewed as positive indicators of success.
Evaluation of school projects shows that awareness has increased of the important influence of exercise and diet on health, and of the damaging effect of harmful substances.

Lessons learned

In areas of deprivation children may have difficulty attending evening sessions during the winter months due to lack of parental support and fears of parents for their safety.

Asian girls rarely stay for activities after school.

Participation can be increased by providing activities in school time, directly after school or during lunch-times.

It is difficult to evaluate to what extent children's perceived attitudes to health will be reflected in their behaviour in the future, i.e. that they believe in the value of regular exercise does not guarantee that they will take regular exercise as an adult.

CASE STUDY 22
FAMILY FUN TRAIL, BARNSLEY

Target groups:	Family groups, toddlers, children aged 5–14 years
Setting:	Urban park
Location:	Barnsley's Dearne Valley Park
Lead organisation:	Health Promotion Service (Barnsley Health Authorities)
Other organisation involved:	Countryside Section, Barnsley M.B.C.
Timescale:	1994 to present
Cost:	£1000 marking the trail
	£500 commemorative T-shirts
	£1000 leaflets, posters and publicity
Source of funding:	Barnsley Health Authority's Health of the Nation funding 1993/94
Contact:	Margaret Crossland
	Health Promotion Service
	Harborough House
	Harborough Hill Road
	Barnsley S71 1BA
	Tel: 01226 770285
Documentation:	Fun Trail map and question sheet
	leaflet
Special features:	due to the non-recurrent nature of the funding the project had to stand alone with minimum future costs; materials were chosen for maximum durability

Background
- The Health Authority invited bids for non-recurrent funding to address Health of the Nation issues.
- The promotion of exercise as easy and enjoyable, by the Health Promotion Service, was one of many bids.

Stated aims
- To encourage 'More People to be More Active, More Often' (this was one of 3 linked projects)
- To raise awareness of the Family Fun Trail and to get people to use it.

Methods employed
- A working group comprising staff from Health Promotion and the Countryside Section of Barnsley MBC together with representatives of South Yorkshire Orienteers designed the trail and map.
- The Countryside Section undertook responsibility for the practicalities of setting up the trail.
- Health Promotion took responsibility for the design of the trail markers, all publicity and the launch. This included much exploratory work with local nursery and primary school children to ensure the suitability of the eventual designs for the markers.
- There are 12 wooden posts around the park each with a plastic disc on top. To cater for all ages each disc is marked with a letter, a picture of an animal and a picture showing a sporting activity.
- Families find each of the markers using appropriate clues and a map, then note down the relevant letter, animal and/or sporting activity. Completed answer sheets can be entered for a draw to win a T-shirt.
- Information on the local orienteering club is provided on the leaflet.

Impact
Too early to assess impact yet.

Possible development
To extend the Fun Trail to disabled young people.

CASE STUDY 23
TREKKERS, EAST SUSSEX

Target group:	Special needs groups of all ages
Setting:	Country Park
Location:	Seven Sisters Country Park, Seaford, East Sussex
Lead organisation:	Trekkers (part of the Cuckmere Cycle Company)
Other organisations:	East Sussex Health Authority, Sports Council
Timescale:	1993 to present
Cost:	£20000 equipment
	£15000 facilities, e.g. disabled toilet, shower, access road
Sources of funding:	Sports Council grant, British Telecom Community Programme, Cuckmere Cycle Company
Contacts:	Kay Muir
	Health Promotion Adviser
	Health Promotion Department
	Avenue House
	The Avenue
	Eastbourne BN21 3XY
	Tel: 01323 430003
Documentation:	report to Sports Council, leaflet and posters

Background

- The project stemmed from the Cuckmere Cycle Company's commitment to provide equal opportunities for all to enjoy cycling as a form of exercise.

Stated aims

- To provide access to the countryside for all.
- To offer a family-orientated cycling centre that caters for all, including groups and schools.

Methods employed

- The Cuckmere Cycle Company researched the needs of disabled people by talking to users and professionals.
- They identified what was needed to provide a service for disabled people and submitted a report to the Sports Council.
- Special bikes were designed which could be ridden by disabled people.
- The centre was opened with five of these specially designed bikes available.
- Open days were held for carers and special needs schools to check that the service offered was appropriate.

Impact

The centre is to be promoted by British Telecom as a centre of excellence for other parks to copy.
Schools use the facility on a regular basis.
There are increasing numbers of people using the specially designed bikes.

Lessons learned

It takes more time than anticipated to deal with the people who come to use the Trekkers facilities.
Running the centre is very labour intensive.

Possible development

Provision of more specialised bikes to cope with demand.

Key recommendations for colleagues

Visit sites to see how they operate, but remember that each location will have its own specific needs.
Always ask the people you are targeting what they would like and need from your facility.

CASE STUDY 24
COVENTRY YOUNG PEOPLE AND SPORT PROGRAMME

Target group:	Young people aged up to 21 years
Settings:	schools, community sports clubs, leisure and sports centres.
Location:	Coventry
Lead organisations:	Sports Council (West Midlands), Coventry City Council Leisure Services, Coventry City Council Education Service
Timescale:	1994 to present
Sources of funding:	Sports Council, Coventry City Council
Contact:	Ken Adamson
	Coventry Support and Advisory Service
	Elm Bank Teachers Centre
	Mile Lane
	Coventry CV1 2LQ
	Tel: 01203 257560
Documentation:	information pack for voluntary sports organisations
	information and advice for governors and head teachers
	information for primary school teachers to support the PE curriculum

Background

- It is important to provide opportunities for participation in physical activity from the earliest years until adulthood.
- There is a need to build firm foundations to enable and encourage young people to take part in sport.
- Young people like to be able to choose from wide range of activities.

Stated aim

To create opportunities for all children and young people in Coventry to participate in sport.

Methods employed

The scheme includes the following objectives:
- development of interest and opportunities for 0–5-year-olds;
- support for the development and delivery of the PE curriculum in primary schools, including the formation of links with other relevant agencies;
- development of out-of-school fun physical activity clubs;
- encouragement of the development of fun activities at break-times in primary schools;
- support for the development and delivery of PE in secondary and community colleges and development of links with sports opportunities in the community;
- development of out-of-school sports opportunities for 11–14-year-olds, 14–16-year-olds and 16–21-year-olds;
- support for the development and delivery of quality coaching for performance-motivated children;
- support for the training of a broad range of people who are in a position to provide sports opportunities for young people;
- development of appropriate sports structures for young people to develop interests in sport (youth leagues, young people's clubs, youth sections in clubs).

Initial developments have focused on the 5–11 age group.

Impact

196 children participate weekly in Fun Fitness Clubs out of school hours.

14 people have been trained to help deliver sports opportunities for 5–11-year-olds.

58 sports clubs have been provided with information packs which encourage the development of participation structures for young people.

101 children participate in after-school sports clubs at schools and sports centres.

115 children participated in a half-term holiday activity programme at various venues.

Lessons learned

A key problem with holiday activities is how children get to sports centres.
Schools are keen to develop physical activity programmes at lunch-times.

Possible developments

Developing training for lunch-time supervisors
Developing further work with external agencies and formulating a coaches network.
Improving the promotion of holiday programmes.

CASE STUDY 25
ROMPERS, ST EDMUNDSBURY

Target group:	Pre-school children aged 1–5 years
Settings:	village halls, community centres, colleges
Location:	St Edmundsbury, Suffolk
Lead organisation:	St Edmundsbury Borough Council Leisure Development Unit
Timescale:	1992 to present
Cost:	£5000 set-up costs
	£7000 per annum ongoing costs
	salary costs for Rompers leader and input from Play Development Officer
Source of funding:	St Edmundsbury Borough Council
Contact:	Justin Wallace
	St Edmundsbury Borough Council
	Angel Hill
	Bury St Edmunds, Suffolk IP33 1XB
	Tel: 01284 757085
Documentation:	information leaflet for parents
	Rompers Record Card, certificate, birthday cards and stickers
Special features:	provides a structured programme for pre-school children

Background

- Existing evidence indicates low levels of activity among young people.
- It was recogised that there is a need to instil the habits of an active lifestyle as early as possible.

Stated aims

- To help lay the foundations of a healthy lifestyle.
- To help give children a headstart in physical education to learn skills and improve confidence.

Methods employed

The Rompers programme:
- aims to develop a child's physical, social and emotional skills through physical activities;
- is progressive and designed to develop children's balance, co-ordination, dexterity and mobility;
- provides children with an opportunity to mix with other children and play in a stimulating environment;
- intersperses short teaching periods with free-play periods to cope with young children's short attention span;
- provides parents with an opportunity to play with their children without the distractions present at home.

Impact

There have been over 9000 visits to Rompers and feedback from parents has been very positive. Rompers is recommended by the local college as a valuable training device for their nursery students.

Lessons learned

Young children learn skills very quickly.
Initial targets had to be revised to take in higher levels of attainment.
Young children require frequent changes in activities as their attention spans are very short.
Most pre-school children appear to have a latent physical ability waiting to be released, and schemes of this nature help nurture this ability.

Possible development

Replication of this scheme by other local authorities.

Key recommendation for colleagues

Take advantage of the scheme developed by St Edmundsbury.

CASE STUDY 26
KEEP FIT AND HEARTY PACK, REDDITCH

Target group:	Young people aged 9–11 years (also adapted for use with younger children)
Setting:	primary schools (predominantly first schools)
Location:	Redditch
Lead organisations:	Action Sport, YMCA
Other organisations:	Healthy Borough, North Worcestershire Health Authority
Timescale:	September 1995 to present
Cost:	£1100 for production of 200 packs
	£5760 per annum staff costs
	£500 administration costs
Sources of funding:	Redditch Borough Council, North Worcestershire Health Authority
Contact:	Paul Stirling
	Sports Development Officer (Action Sport)
	c/o Abbey Stadium
	Birmingham Road
	Redditch B97 6EJ
	Tel: 01527 64676
Documentation:	Keep Fit and Hearty Pack
Special features:	Playfun sessions are free as it was felt that recreationally deprived schools often have children with the greatest social problems

Background
- There is increasing concern about the low levels of physical activity among children.

Stated aims
- To promote and develop healthy lifestyles amongst 5–11-year-olds in Redditch.
- To encourage children to make exercise a regular and frequent activity.
- To help children understand the relationship between physical activity and health.

Methods employed
Schools are provided with the Keep Fit and Hearty Pack, designed for years 7 and 8, which aims:
- to help teachers impart knowledge on health-related topics and physical activity;
- to reinforce positive attitudes to physical activity and a healthy lifestyle among staff and students;
- to provide local support for teachers to help foster positive attitudes towards active healthy living;
- to complement the National Curriculum.

After-school Playfun sessions have been set up for 5–11-year-olds. Sessions:
- are run by appropriately qualified staff;
- promote physical activity in a fun way, with team games, circuits and exercise to music.

Impact
500 children per week currently participate in Playfun sessions.
Some children have reduced weight and there is evidence of improvement in problems associated with asthma.
There is a waiting list of schools wishing to join the scheme.

Lessons learned
A more extensive evaluation is needed to measure outcomes.

Possible development
Developing the scheme to include older age ranges, i.e. 11–14-year-olds and 14+ years.

Key recommendation for colleagues
Make sure that partnerships with other agencies are formed to develop schemes.

CASE STUDY 27
MOBILE FITNESS FACTOR, DUDLEY

Target group:	Children and young people of all abilities aged 7–17 years
Setting:	schools
Location:	Dudley Metropolitan Borough
Lead organisations:	Dudley Priority Health NHS Trust, Education Department, Community Development Unit, Leisure Services, Health Promotion 95
Timescale:	1992 to present
Cost:	£140,000 1992–1995
	£43,000 1996–1997
Sources of funding:	1991–1994 central government's urban development programme
	1994–1995 Leisure Services, Community Development Unit, Dudley Health Authority
	1996–1997 Dudley Health Authority
Contact:	Dean Hill
	Health Promotion Department
	Dudley Health Authority
	Shousters House
	Ridge Hill
	Brierley Hill Road
	Stourbridge
	West Midlands DY8 5ST
	Tel: 01384 456111
Documentation:	Dinosaur Fitlife Plan and certificates

Background

There was a desire to encourage and enable the people of Dudley to be more active, more often.

Stated aim

Projects targeted at young people aimed to increase local levels of activity amongst 7–18-year-olds.

Methods employed

Primary schools
- A whole-school assembly presents a play featuring Deano the Dinosaur and introducing the Fitlife plan.
- The Fitlife plan provides advice on physical activity and healthy eating and sets goals for the next 4 weeks, with sections for children to record their progress.
- Complementing the assembly is an activity day to motivate the children to be more active. The whole school completes a circuit-based activity which aims to exercise children and to explain what happens to their blood during exercise.
- On completion of the one-month period, Deano the Dinosaur returns to the school and certificates are given to all children who have completed the Fitlife plan.

Secondary schools
- Work is based on a supply and demand system.
- Activities have included an 8-week block of circuit training, health-focus weeks, mountain biking and 'Gladiator' sessions.

Impact

Over 5000 schools have been involved in the project.
An average of 73% of Fitlife plans are completed and returned.
Due to the popularity of the project, and the appeal of the dinosaur character, Deano has been adopted for other school-based initiatives such as PE lessons and work on safety in play. A walk safely to school pilot scheme is being carried out with dinosaur footprints indicating safe crossing points.

Lessons learned

The project needs multi-skilled staff who can deliver to individuals of any age, sex, ethnic group etc.

The project works very well in socially and economically deprived areas where people are unwilling to pay to participate in leisure centre activities.

Possible developments

Project developments for young people planned for the next 3 years include:

- producing a resource pack for primary teachers;
- developing assembly presentations and health-related fitness days in the primary sector;
- piloting an inter-school walking competition for 7–11-year-olds, to be held bi-annually;
- organising one big inter-agency event;
- contributing to newsletters for children and young people;
- carrying out needs assessments of young people aged 11–21 years, teachers of this age group and youth workers;
- responding to the needs assessments by providing appropriate resources;
- providing activity sessions for young people with special needs.

CASE STUDY 28
EXERCISE ROADSHOW, SUNDERLAND

Target group:	primary school children aged 7–11 years
Setting:	primary schools
Location:	Sunderland
Lead organisations:	Priority Healthcare Wearside NHS Trust, Health Promotion and Education Services Department
Timescale:	August 1995 to present
Cost:	£1000 training for staff
	£1000 booklet production
	£2000 equipment and resources
Source of funding:	Sunderland Health Authority
Contact:	Marc Hopkinson
	Priority Health Care Wearside
	Health Promotion and Education Services
	Monkwearmouth Hospital
	Newcastle Road
	Sunderland SR5 1NB
	Tel: 0191 565 6256 ext. 48251
Documentation:	booklet detailing aims and objectives, games played etc.
Special features:	children are given the opportunity to make suggestions/criticisms of programme content during the Roadshow allowing more effective evaluation

Background

- Awareness of research evidence indicating that young people are becoming less active.
- A district-wide Energise Strategy has already been established, spearheaded by Priority Healthcare Wearside. The strategy:
  - works on the concept of spiral education;
  - aims to co-ordinate exercise provision across all key stages to all schools in the district of Sunderland;
  - seeks to work in close collaboration with other exercise and nutrition providers.

Stated aims

- To encourage increased levels of physical activity within primary schools.
- To increase knowledge among primary school teachers of the benefits of physical activity

Methods employed

- The project is offered to schools and a selected number of schools are chosen to take part in the Roadshow.
- The Roadshow has been designed to encourage primary school children to participate in and enjoy physical activity whilst also increasing their knowledge of the benefits of physical activity.
- Roadshow sessions are given by suitably qualified personnel.
- Children are provided with activities not normally used in a typical PE lesson, which could be organised and carried out at school or home by the children themselves.
- Teachers are offered new, fun ideas which satisfy National Curriculum requirements, for use in PE lessons,.
- Resources for the games are provided, with a selection of these remaining in the school to encourage further development.
- A booklet showing a selection of games is distributed to schools.
- Teachers receive training in safe exercise.
- A range of media is used to promote the project in relation to improved lifestyle.

Impact

74% of schools were interested in taking part in the Roadshow.
A pilot programme was delivered to schools.
Evaluation is not yet completed.

CASE STUDY 29
GET ACTIVE PROGRAMME

Target groups:	People of all ages with learning disabilities
Settings:	Gateway Clubs, day and residential centres, schools, leisure centres, fitness centres, universities, Link projects
Location:	England, Wales and Northern Ireland
Lead organisations:	National Federation of Gateway Clubs, The Manchester Metropolitan University (MMU), Department of Exercise and Sport Science
Timescale:	1990 to present
Cost:	£10000 initial costs
	£7500 ongoing costs
	£8000 tutor-training costs
Sources of funding:	Sports Council, the Foundation for Sports and the Arts, Key Finance Ltd, Department for Education and Employment
Contacts:	Jack Gorman *The* Manchester Metropolitan University Crewe and Alsager Faculty Department of Exercise and Sport Science Hassall Road Alsager ST7 2HL Tel: 0161 247 5540 Karen Nicol National Federation of Gateway Clubs 117 Golden Lane London EC1Y 0RT Tel: 0171 696 5590
Documentation:	resource material for tutors leaflets for participants tutor-training course documentation
Special features:	materials are designed to encourage and allow programmes to be constructed easily and presented visually for an individual and/or group

Background
- There was an awareness of the high profile of healthier living for the general population.
- It was recognised that for people with learning disabilities, keeping fit and finding good exercise opportunities is not easy.
- The need to enable learning-disabled people to develop a healthier lifestyle was identified.
- The Mental Impairment and General Health Training Programme (MIGHT) was conceived and developed by MMU and a local fitness centre, to train carers in promoting fitness programmes for people with learning disabilities.
- The National Federation for Gateway Clubs suggested a programme of collaboration, and the MIGHT programme developed into the Get Active Programme (GAP).

Stated aims
- To improve the health and fitness of the identified population.
- To develop sufficient levels of fitness to enable participation in other activities.
- To train carers and other interested people to a level of competence in the use of the GAP resource materials.
- To promote the use of the GAP resource materials in Gateway Clubs and other target population settings.
- To evaluate the effectiveness of the Get Active Programme.

Methods employed
- Initial research used informal interviews with carers and the target group to collect data.
- Research helped identify needs and possible ways forward.
- Resource materials were created for tutors and target groups.
- A tutor-training course was developed and delivered, then revised accordingly.
- Resource materials are currently being evaluated and revised.
- A video to assist safe exercise is in the process of being produced.

Impact

A pool of knowledgeable, confident tutors is being created with the resources to effect change.
Informal feedback reveals that the programme is becoming increasingly successful in achieving its aims.
The Get Active Programme is included in undergraduate studies.

Lessons learned

It is important to clarify the aims of the project by talking to appropriate people (particularly the target group).
It is important to ensure adequate funding or sponsorship is available to enable appropriate stage planning.
It is important to produce quality materials which can be readily communicated.
It is important to be prepared to evaluate and where necessary go back to the drawing board.
First solutions were rarely the final solutions.

Possible developments

A major research project to investigate effectiveness.
Development of activity-specific resource materials.
Seminar presentations to appropriate groups to promote greater awareness.

Key recommendations for colleagues

Talk with target groups and others to identify needs.
Clarify aims and objectives before seeking funding or sponsorship.
Develop a sound working group and an extensive network.
Given positive outcomes from market research, persevere when seeking funding or sponsorship.

CASE STUDY 30
YOUTH SPORTS DEVELOPMENT PROJECT, GLOUCESTERSHIRE

Target group:	young people aged 11–25 years
Settings:	youth centres, colleges of higher education, schools and sports clubs
Location:	Gloucestershire
Lead organisation:	Gloucestershire Youth and Community Service
Other organisations:	Sports Council (South West), Cheltenham and Gloucester College of Higher Education
Timescale:	March 1994 to February 1997
Sources of funding:	Gloucestershire Youth and Community Service, Sports Council (South West), Cheltenham and Gloucester College of Higher Education, commercial sponsorship for individual projects, Sportsmatch
Contact:	Mandy Hymers
	Youth Sports Development Officer
	Gloucestershire Youth and Community Service
	Chequers Bridge Centre
	Painswick Road
	Gloucester GL4 6PR
	Tel: 01452 425420
Documentation:	directory of local sports opportunities for disabled people
	leaflets on coaching courses
	Tewkesbury Borough Youth Sports Action Plan
	Women's Football Development Plan for Gloucestershire
	Table Tennis Development Plan for Gloucestershire
Special features:	links are developing to provide opportunities in and outside of the school environment

Background

- The lack of good quality sports opportunities for young people within the youth service was identified.
- The idea was formulated to appoint a specific sports development officer.
- Negotiations with two other partners were carried out to identify funding, develop objectives, outline a job description and appoint the officer.

Stated aim

To provide, promote and develop good quality sports opportunities for young people aged 11–25 years in Gloucestershire, particularly young people within the youth and community service.

Methods employed

- A programme of sports training courses for youth workers and students was set up, including C.C.P.R. Community Sports Leaders Award and National Governing Body and National Coaching Foundation courses.
- Sports-specific development programmes were initiated to develop interest in focus sports by youth workers, and to encourage them to provide a range of opportunities which are sustainable in the long term.
- Information was updated and sports provision highlighted to encourage involvement and motivate young people.
- Knowledge and expertise was provided to support youth workers.
- A Youth Sports Action Plan for Tewkesbury Borough was researched and produced in partnership with students and Tewkesbury Borough Council. This provides a focus for the whole community to work together to develop sport for young people.
- External training and placement opportunities were provided for students at Cheltenham and Gloucester College of Higher Education, as a support to academic programmes and for students' personal development.

Impact

More young people are involved in sport within youth centres.

The quality of sports provision has greatly improved. In the first 18 months, 85 qualifications were gained by 58 youth and community service staff.

Much positive feedback has been received and all partners are hopeful that funding will be made available for the post to continue after the initial 3-year period.

There is now county co-ordination of sports training courses, with a regular programme of courses available county wide.

Lessons learned

Sport is perceived within the youth and community service as being competitive.

Sport can be used within the youth and community service for the provision of social education, as well as for its own sake, if the youth and community service and the local community both take steps to develop partnerships.

Possible developments

Continuation of similar projects to consolidate the good practice currently set up.

The development of work as an integral part of the youth and community service.

Focus on more specific developments for girls and young women, disabled young people and young people from minority ethnic groups.

Appendices

APPENDIX 1

KEY NATIONAL ORGANISATIONS

A co-ordinated approach between the various relevant organisations at both a national and local level is needed if promotions aimed at encouraging young people to be active are to be effective. The following organisations are primarily concerned with influencing decisions and policy.

National government departments

Department of Health

- Has a core responsibility to initiate appropriate action for the promotion of physical activity within government.
- Will liaise with the Physical Activity Task Force to monitor levels of physical activity, consider ways of promoting physical activity and identify relevant research needs.

The NHS Executive, which is within the Department of Health, has a responsibility to:

- network good practice in implementing and monitoring progress towards Health of the Nation targets.

Department for National Heritage

- Promotes the overall interests of sport within the government.
- Aims to increase the opportunities for sport and recreation both for the champions and the general public through the provision of facilities and opportunities.
- Has been working with government departments to promote the role of schools in establishing an active lifestyle from a young age.

Department for Education

- Has a responsibility for the implementation and assessment of the Physical Education National Curriculum in schools.

- Is involved in supporting the provision of physical education in-service courses and in providing support and guidance to schools on sharing their facilities with the local community.

Department of Environment

- Sets the planning framework within which local authorities are encouraged to develop policies to promote physical activity.

- Provides guidance on increasing the number of short journeys made on foot, and advice on helping cyclists.

Addressing the needs of pedestrians and cyclists is also a concern of the Department of Transport.

The Health Education Authority

- Is co-ordinating the national physical activity campaign Active for Life.

- Is involved in working with other national and local agencies to support the development and implementation of physical activity initiatives.

- Has funded a number of important projects concerned with the promotion of physical activity to young people, in particular the HEA Health and Physical Education Project (for secondary schools) and the Happy Heart Project (for primary schools).

- Continues to provide support for the promotion of physical activity among young people.

- Is currently involved in co-ordinating the European Network of Health-Promoting Schools Project.

The Institute of Leisure and Amenity Management

The Institute of Leisure and Amenity Management (ILAM) represents over 7000 leisure professionals from the public, private, voluntary and commercial sectors. Their commitment to improving opportunities for young people to pursue physical activity is highlighted by:

- the policy position statement on Children's Play and Recreation, which was produced in association with a number of other relevant bodies including the National Playing Fields Association, the National Children's Bureau and the National Voluntary Council for Children's Play. This policy advocates the need for a national strategy for children's play and recreation and highlights key issues and common objectives for future work.

ILAM also:

- promotes the important role that leisure has to play in the redress of youth crime, and has produced a policy position statement on this issue.

The National Playing Fields Association

- Has a responsibility for acquiring, protecting and improving playing fields, playgrounds and play space where they are most needed, in particular for children of all ages and those with a disability.
- Provides an advisory service and a range of publications on play, sport and recreational facilities.
- Is a leading authority on design, layout, improvement and safety of playgrounds, playing fields and other playing space.

The Countryside Commission

- Has a statutory duty to advise government and others about countryside conservation and recreation.
- Aims to enable and encourage others such as local authorities (who are their main partners), voluntary bodies, farmers and landowners, and the business community to achieve practical results on the ground.
- Has a commitment to 'secure opportunities for people to enjoy and appreciate the countryside for open-air recreation'.
- Is already committed to ensure that high quality opportunities exist for extensive journeys on foot, horseback and cycle.
- Has proposed in a recent consultation document that future work could include supporting the creation of new open spaces for local recreation, and raising awareness of countryside and recreation opportunities.

OTHER NATIONAL ORGANISATIONS

There are a number of national organisations who have developed nationally recognised schemes and activities which can be adopted at a local level.

British Heart Foundation (BHF)

Relevant aspects of their work include:

- the production of a newsletter for teenagers which looks at the benefits of physical activity;
- the production of a pack on exercise and heart health for those aged 7–11 years (*At the Heart of Education*);

- the co-ordination of the Jump Rope for Heart programme, which can be used by schools and community groups;

- numerous local and national sponsored physical-activity events;

- the development of an Active Schools promotion to focus on providing more appropriate physical-activity opportunities for young people within and outside of school. This will provide schools with practical advice and ideas.

Physical Education Association of the United Kingdom (PEA UK)

PEA UK has undergone reorganisation, but currently the Association:

- provides support for those involved in teaching physical education;

- provides a range of in-service training;

- produces a quarterly journal for members, a research journal and a newsletter specifically for primary school teachers providing valuable advice and support.

Sports Council

The Sports Council:

- has provided continued support for the development of initiatives aimed at improving sporting opportunities for young people;

- aims to improve sporting opportunities for young people within schools and the community through the National Junior Sport Programme and the Youth Sport Trust and Sports Council's TOP Programme.

The National Junior Sport Programme

This attempts to embrace all quality sports provision for young people in schools, in community settings and in governing body structures within a high-profile national programme. New initiatives will be developed to fit 'gaps' in provision.

The TOP Programme

This will be co-ordinated nationally by the Youth Sport Trust and Sports Council and be delivered locally. It includes four programmes to be delivered in schools and the community:

- **TOP Play** aims to nurture 4–9-year-old's enthusiasm for activity with core skills and fun sport;

- **TOP Sport** introduces sport and games to 7–11-year-olds;

- **Champion Coaching** aims to increase performance in 11–14-year-olds;

- **TOP Club** helps sports clubs to build a future in sport for children of all ages, including devising a junior development plan and making links with schools.

A national training programme will be provided for lunch-time organisers, leaders, parents, coaches and enthusiastic volunteers to help children enter and stay in sporting activities.

National governing bodies of sport

Many national governing bodies of sport:

- provide support to schools and community organisations;
- have introduced modified versions of games which are more appropriate for young people;
- have appointed national and/or regional youth development officers to provide help and support.

The Exercise Association of England has recently been established as a national governing body and has identified young people as one of their target groups. A standing committee is currently examining existing physical-activity initiatives for young people and identifying gaps in current provision with a view to developing relevant initiatives in the future.

APPENDIX 2

KEY LOCAL ORGANISATIONS

There are numerous local organisations who can provide practical help at a local level. Some of these will also have an influence on policy and decision-making at a local level.

Regional and District Health Authorities

District Health Authorities (DHAs):

- have a responsibility to assess the health status and needs of their population and to secure the provision of health care to meet these needs;
- may wish to purchase a service to address a need for increased activity levels among young people in the district.

Regional Health Authorities:

- have become regional offices for the NHS Executive;
- have a responsibility to move forward NHS national priorities including those set out in the Health of the Nation.

Health promotion services:

- in the past were based in DHAs with support from a regional level;
- at a local level may now be relocated within one or more NHS Trusts or within the public health function in DHAs.

Many health promotion officers work to promote physical activity within schools and the local community, and in some cases they are appointed with a specific remit for physical-activity promotion. Health promotion officers:

- tend to act as trainers and networkers rather than doers;
- are often involved in co-ordinating physical-activity promotions for young people;
- provide support and advice on physical activity and arrange training opportunities.

Local authorities

Local authorities have a key role to play in the promotion of physical activity to young people through their leisure and recreation function. The roles and responsibilities of leisure and recreation can include:

- the general promotion of leisure and recreation;
- a responsibility for targeting a specific group such as young people;

- a responsibility for promoting leisure and recreation in a particular locality;

- a responsibility for promoting a specific activity or sport.

Local authorities have a significant influence on the availability of physical-activity opportunities for young people and can be a major partner in local partnerships to promote physical activity. Potential areas in which local authorities can have a particular impact are:

- through co-ordinating local activity opportunities for young people;

- developing strategic plans aimed at promoting physical activity to young people;

- through the creation of appropriate structures and the promotion of relevant partnerships;

- by providing appropriate leisure facilities and opportunities within these facilities;

- by appointing sports development officers with a remit for promoting physical activity among young people;

- through the development of safe and appealing parks and playgrounds.

Local education authorities

Many LEAs still have physical advisers and inspectors and LEAs are a key partner in the implementation of any physical activity initiatives involving schools, and in providing support and guidance for schools and teachers.

Sports Council regional offices

Many of the Sports Council's regional offices have developed specific initiatives for young people including:

- the appointment of sports development officers with a remit focusing on young people;

- school/clubs link schemes (Sports Council West Midlands Region);

- the development of youth sport action groups/Plans (Sports Council West Midlands Region, Sports Council South West Region);

- the establishment of school/community links (Sports Council South West Region).

Sports clubs and associations

Sports clubs and associations offer a potential network of activity opportunities outside of schools. In order to effectively encourage more participation in these opportunities there is a need for:

- the development of specific junior sections and development plans;

- the provision of support and encouragement for young people of all standards;
- the initiation of links with local schools.

Voluntary and community groups

A variety of voluntary and community groups provide opportunities for young people to participate in physical activity, and these are particularly important as they are likely to be more accessible.

Youth services

Statutory and voluntary youth services, organisations and clubs can:

- provide opportunities for young people to take part in physical activity;
- provide opportunities for young people themselves to organise and lead activities.

Youth Clubs UK are developing 'Sports Fair' which aims 'to promote among young people, an active attitude that can find expression in a wide range of quality youth sports experiences through a youth service linked structure, delivered locally and co-ordinated nationally'.

Institutes of higher education/universities

Institutes of higher education have a potentially significant influence on physical activity provision for young people. They:

- are responsible for the training of teachers who are delivering physical education in schools;
- provide relevant in-service training opportunities for teachers and a range of other professionals;
- often have the expertise to carry out appropriate research;
- can be involved in monitoring relevant physical-activity projects.

APPENDIX 3

TRAINING OPPORTUNITIES

The Central Council of Physical Recreation (CCPR)

co-ordinates the:

- **Junior Sports Leader Award,** which helps young people aged 14–16 years to develop leadership skills which can be applied to a variety of sporting activities;
- **Community Sports Leader Award,** to enable those over 16 years of age to provide voluntary assistance alongside qualified coaches or teachers;
- **Hanson Award,** for those who have leadership experience and wish to develop their interest in sport and also to pursue training in administration or in areas of special need.

The National Coaching Foundation

Offers modules on working with young people which are appropriate for coaches and teachers.

National governing bodies of sport

Most organise courses of varying levels for those interested in introducing a sport to young people.

The Physical Education Association UK

Organises an in-service training scheme which includes both distance-learning materials and short courses on a range of subject areas.

The Central YMCA (Training and development unit)

has developed:

- First level – a series of qualifications in health-related exercise. The Core Module 'Personal Exercise Programmes' is designed to fulfil the Health-related Exercise Requirements of the National Curriculum for Physical Education at Key Stage 4 (age 14–16). The Core Module can also be linked to GCSE and A-level course work;
- a Basic Certificate in the Teaching of Exercise to Music (RSA-approved) for those wishing to lead exercise to music classes;

- a Fitness Training Course for leaders wishing to teach weight training and circuit training;
- a range of other specialist training courses.

Youth Clubs UK

Will provide training for youth leaders as part of the Sports Fair initiative to help them introduce young people to physical activity.

The Youth Sport Trust

Provides training related to their TOP programme for lunch-time organisers, leaders, parents, coaches and enthusiastic volunteers.

APPENDIX 4

FURTHER READING

For those who want to follow up particular aspects of work with young people, the following sources will provide additional information and reading.

Armstrong, N. & Welshman, J. (1994) 'Todays Children; Fitness, Fatness and Physical Activity', *Education and Health*. vol. 12, no. 5, pp. 65–69.

Biddle, S. J. & Fox, K. (1988) 'The child's perspective in Physical Education – Teaching Psychosocial Development through Teaching and Coaching, *British Journal of Physical Education*.

Cale, L. and Almond, L. (1992) 'Children's Activity Levels: A review of studies conducted on British Children', *Physical Education Review*. vol. 15, no. 2, pp. 111–118.

Cheung and Richmond (eds.) (1995) 'Child Health, Nutrition and Physical Activity', *Human Kinetics*, Illinois

Corbin, C.B., Pangrazi, R.P. and Welk, G.J. (1994) 'Towards an understanding of appropriate physical activity levels for youth', *Physical Activity and Research Digest*. Series 1, no. 8, pp. 1–8. President's Council on Fitness and Sport, USA.

Fox K. (1994) 'Research Perspectives on Children's Competence and Achievement in Physical Education and Sport', *British Journal of Physical Education*. vol. 25, no. 2, pp. 20–22.

HEA *Promoting Physical Activity – Guidance for commissioners, purchasers and providers* (1995). Health Education Authority, London.

Kemper, H.C.G. (1994) 'The Natural History of Physical Activity and Aerobic Fitness in Teenagers', *Advances in Exercise Adherence* (ed. Dishman, R. K.). pp. 293–318. Human Kinetics, Champaign, Illinois.

Moving On – international perspectives on promoting physical activity (1995). Health Education Authority, London.

'Physical Activity' (1995) *Health Update*. vol. 5. Health Education Authority, London.

Riddoch, C.J. and Boreham, C.A.G., (1995) 'The Health Related Activity of Children', *Sports Medicine*. vol. 19, no. 2, pp. 86–102.

Sallis, J.F. and Patrick, K. (1994) 'Physical Activity guidelines for adolescents: consensus statement', *Paediatric Exercise Science*. vol. 6, no. 4, pp. 302–314.

Sport – Raising the Game (1995), Department of National Heritage, London.

Young People and Sport in England (1984). Sports Council, London.

Young People and Sport – Policy and Frameworks for Action Sports Council (1993). Sports Council, London.

APPENDIX 5

USEFUL ADDRESSES

British Heart Foundation
Education Department
14 Fitzhardinge Street
London W1H 4DH
Tel 0171 935 0185

Central Council of Physical Recreation
Francis House
Francis Street
London SW1P 1DE
Tel 0171 828 3163

Central YMCA (Training and Development Unit)
112 Great Russell Street
London WC1B 3NQ
Tel 0171 343 1850

Countryside Commission
John Dower House
Crescent Place
Cheltenham
Gloucestershire GL50 3RA
Tel 01242 521381

Exercise Association of England
Unit 4
Angel Gate
City Road
London EC1V 2PT
Tel 0171 278 0811

Health Education Authority
Physical Activity Project
Hamilton House
Mabledon Place
London WC1H 9TX
Tel 0171 413 2637

Loughborough University
Exercise and Health Group
Department of Physical Education, Sports Science and Recreation Management
Loughborough University
Ashby Road
Loughborough
Leicestershire LE11 3TU
Tel 01509 223259

Institute of Leisure Amenity Management (I.L.A.M.)
I.L.A.M. House
Lower Basildon
Reading
Berkshire RG8 9NE
Tel 01491 874222

National Coaching Foundation
114 Cardigan Road
Leeds LS6 3BJ
Tel 0113 274 4802

National Governing Bodies of Sport

Details of the National Governing Bodies of Sport and their activities can be obtained from the Central Council of Physical Recreation (See p.106)

National Playing Fields Association
25 Ovington Square
London SW3 1LQ
Tel 0171 584 6445

Physical Education Association of the United Kingdom
Suite 5
10 Churchill Square
Kings Hill
West Malling
Kent ME19 4DU
Tel 01732 875888

Sports Council
16 Upper Woburn Place
London WC1H 0QP
Tel 0171 273 1500

Youth Clubs U.K.
11 St Brides Street
London EC4A 4AS
Tel 0171 353 2366

Youth Sports Trust
Rutland Building
Loughborough University
Loughborough
Leicestershire LE11 3TU
Tel 01509 228293